lonely planet

Pocket
CHICAGO
TOP SIGHTS • LOCAL LIFE • MADE EASY

In This Book

QuickStart Guide

Your keys to understanding the city – we help you decide what to do and how to do it

Need to Know
Tips for a smooth trip

Neighborhoods
What's where

Explore Chicago

The best things to see and do, neighborhood by neighborhood

Top Sights
Make the most of your visit

Local Life
The insider's city

The Best of Chicago

The city's highlights in handy lists to help you plan

Best Walks
See the city on foot

Chicago's Best...
The best experiences

Survival Guide

Tips and tricks for a seamless, hassle-free city experience

Getting Around
Travel like a local

Essential Information
Including where to stay

Our selection of the city's best places to eat, drink and experience:

◎ **Sights**

✴ **Eating**

⦿ **Drinking**

✪ **Entertainment**

🅐 **Shopping**

These symbols give you the vital information for each listing:

- ☎ Telephone Numbers
- ⊙ Opening Hours
- Ⓟ Parking
- ⊖ Nonsmoking
- @ Internet Access
- 🛜 Wi-Fi Access
- 🥗 Vegetarian Selection
- 📖 English-Language Menu

- 🚼 Family-Friendly
- 🐾 Pet-Friendly
- 🚌 Bus
- ⛴ Ferry
- Ⓜ Metro
- Ⓢ Subway
- 🚋 Tram
- 🚆 Train

Find each listing quickly on maps for each neighborhood:

Bar Hemingway

16 ⦿ Map p233, B2

Legend has it that Hemiself, wielding a machine ...rate this timber-pan ...ered bar during ... showpiece is a ...en by Papa ar town. Dress s.com; Hôtel Rit ; ⊙6.30pm-2a

6 ◎ Plac

QuickStart Guide **7**

Explore Chicago **21**

Worth a Trip:

The Best of Chicago 125

Chicago's Best Walks

Chicago's Best ...

Survival Guide 145

QuickStart Guide

Welcome to Chicago

Take cloud-scraping architecture, lakefront beaches and world-class museums, stir in wild comedy, fret-bending guitars and very hefty pizza, and you've got a town that won't let you down. The city center is a steely wonder, but it's Chicago's mural-splashed neighborhoods – with their inventive storefront restaurants, fringe theaters and sociable dive bars – that really blow you away.

Blues musician Eddie Shaw performs at Kingston Mines (p77)
DANIEL LADENHAUF/500PX ©

Chicago Top Sights

Art Institute of Chicago (p28)

Masterpieces from around the globe hang in the vast marble halls, including a whopping collection of impressionist and post-impressionist paintings. Grant Wood's *American Gothic* and Edward Hopper's *Nighthawks* are other highlights.

Millennium Park (p24)

It's the playful heart of the city, shining with whimsical public art. Go ahead, touch the silvery smoothness of 'the Bean' and get splashed by the human gargoyles of Jaume Plensa's *Crown Fountain* (pictured).

Willis Tower (p30)

The 103rd-floor observatory in Chicago's loftiest skyscraper puts you way up in the clouds. The glass-floored ledges hanging out in midair are every bit as scary as you imagine.

Wrigley Field
(p80)

A tangible sense of history comes alive at the 1914 ballpark, thanks to the hand-turned scoreboard, iconic neon entrance sign, legendary curses and time-honored traditions that infuse games played here.

Field Museum of Natural History
(p112)

The collection here is mammoth and all encompassing, ranging from the world's largest Tyrannosaurus rex and the world's largest (stuffed) man-eating lion to a slew of mummies, gemstones and totem poles.

360° Chicago
(p56)

The observatory unfurls a heck of a view, 94 stories up in the sky, right by the lake. If that's not enough, stand at the window that tilts you out over the ground.

Lincoln Park
(p68)

Chicago's largest park is where locals come out to play. They jog the leafy pathways, swim at the beach, watch the zoo animals or just snooze under a shady tree.

Navy Pier (p44)

Stretching away from the skyline and into the blue of Lake Michigan, half-mile-long Navy Pier is Chicago's most-visited attraction. Its charms revolve around the cool breezes, sweet views and crackling fireworks shows.

Museum of Contemporary Art
(p58)

You never know what will be showing from the collection, but it'll probably be unorthodox and boundary-smashing. Minimalist, surrealist and conceptual photography works are the strong suits.

Chicago Local Life

Insider tips to help you find the real city

After checking off Chicago's top sights, seek out the bohemian jazz clubs, brainy bookstores, doughnut bakeries and arty shops that make up the locals' Windy City. Count on neon-bathed dive bars and cool galleries also popping up.

Mixing It Up in Andersonville & Uptown (p86)

▶ LGBT pubs
▶ Al Capone's speakeasy

Multicultural Andersonville offers convivial gastropubs, old curiosity shops and gay and lesbian saloons. Around the corner in Uptown, Chicago's Vietnamese community clusters on Argyle St, while barflies and jazz fans mingle at the Green Mill lounge.

A Night Out in Logan Square (p98)

▶ Neighborhood bars
▶ Indie shops

Join artists and stylish types chowing down in boisterous taverns, hoisting suds in industrial brewpubs and listening to tunes in hepcat music clubs. Crafty shops and rock-and-roll galleries make appearances, too.

West Loop Wander (p102)

▶ Hip cafes
▶ Contemporary galleries

Walk around the forklifts and meatpacking warehouses to discover funky art galleries, hidden delis and gourmet doughnut shops. Then learn about local labor history over a microbrew and sniff out a baklava-wafting Greek cafe.

A Bookish Day in Hyde Park (p122)

▶ Scholarly bookstores
▶ Famous architecture

You can learn a lot walking around the neighborhood that's home to the erudite University of Chicago. Spend the day where Nobel laureates and other locals do, in scholarly bookstores and smart museums, cafeterias and hip music halls.

Wolfbait & B-girls (p99)

Green Mill (p87)

Other great places to experience the city like a local:

Daley Plaza (p40)

SummerDance (p120)

Sweet Maple Cafe (p108)

The 606 (p92)

Flo (p94)

Hendrickx Belgian Bread Crafter (p64)

Happy Village (p95)

Mia Francesca (p84)

Una Mae's (p97)

Green Door Tavern (p52)

Chicago Day Planner

Day One

You might as well dive right in with the big stuff in the Loop. Take a boat or walking tour with the **Chicago Architecture Foundation** (p144) and ogle the most sky-scraping collection of buildings the US has to offer. Saunter over to **Millennium Park** (p24) to see 'the Bean' reflect the skyline and to splash under Crown Fountain's human gargoyles.

Stay in the Loop for lunch. The **Gage** (p36) and **Seven Lions** (p36) dish up pub grub with inventive twists. Explore the **Art Institute of Chicago** (p28), the nation's second-largest art museum, holding masterpieces aplenty. Then head over to **Willis Tower** (p30), zip up to the 103rd floor and step out onto the glass-floored ledge. Yes, it is a long way down.

The West Loop parties in the evening. Walk along Randolph St and take your pick of hot-chef restaurants, such as **Little Goat** (p106), **Girl and the Goat** (p106) or **Avec** (p106). Bars are chockablock too. **RM Champagne Salon** (p108) provides a pretty refuge for a sip.

Day Two

Begin in the Near North with a stroll on Michigan Ave – aka the **Magnificent Mile** (p48) – where big-name department stores ka-ching in a glittering row. Mosey over to **Navy Pier** (p44). Take a spin on the Ferris wheel and grab lunch at the pier outpost of **Giordano's** (p45).

Spend the afternoon at the South Loop's Museum Campus (the water taxi from Navy Pier is a fine way to get there). Miles of aisles of dinosaurs and gemstones stuff the **Field Museum** (p112). Fish and turtles swim in the kiddie-mobbed **Shedd Aquarium** (p116). Meteorites and supernovas are on view at the **Adler Planetarium** (p116).

Hop the Blue Line to Damen for a meal at retro diner **Dove's Luncheonette** (p92) in Wicker Park. Wander along Milwaukee Ave and take your pick of booming bars, indie rock clubs and hipster shops. **Quimby's** (p96) shows the local spirit; the zine bookstore is a linchpin of Chicago's underground culture. **Double Door** (p95) and **Hideout** (p95) are sweet spots to catch a bad-ass band.

Short on time?
We've arranged Chicago's must-sees into these day-by-day itineraries to make sure you see the very best of the city in the time you have available.

Day Three

☀ Get some fresh air this morning. Dip your toes in Lake Michigan at **North Avenue Beach** (p72). Amble northward through the sprawling greenery of **Lincoln Park** (p68). Stop at **Lincoln Park Zoo** (p72) to see lions and tigers and bears (the polar kind). Pop into **Lincoln Park Conservatory** (p72) to smell exotic blooms.

☀ Make your way north to **Wrigley Field** (p80) for an afternoon baseball game. The atmospheric, century-old ballpark hosts the woefully cursed Cubs. Afterward have a beer at **Gingerman** (p83) or one of the many rowdy bars that circle the stadium.

☽ Head to Andersonville & Uptown in the evening. Hmm, mussels and frites at **Hopleaf** (p87), or southern-style chicken and dumplings at **Big Jones** (p87)? Andersonville has several fine taverns to hang out at and sink a pint. Jazz hounds can venture onward to the **Green Mill** (p87), a timeless venue to hear jazz, watch a poetry slam or swill a martini. Al Capone used to groove on it.

Day Four

☀ You can learn a lot in Hyde Park. The **Museum of Science & Industry** (p123) isn't kidding around with its acres of exhibits. There's a German U-boat, mock tornado and exquisite doll house for starters. University bookstores such as **Seminary Co-op** (p123) and **Powell's** (p123) offer shelves of weighty tomes. Architecture buffs can tour **Robie House** (p123), Frank Lloyd Wright's Prairie-style masterpiece. Have lunch at **Valois Cafeteria** (p123), Obama's old hangout.

☀ See what's going on in the chi chi Gold Coast. There's boutique shopping, of course. The **Museum of Contemporary Art** (p58) always has something odd and provocative showing. And you can't leave the 'hood without getting high. For that, ascend to the 94th-floor observatory at **360° Chicago** (p56) or the 96th-floor **Signature Lounge** (p64).

☽ Spend the evening among locals in hip-happening Logan Sq. Sip whiskey while waiting for a table at **Longman & Eagle** (p99). Knock back slurpable beers at **Revolution Brewing** (p99). See what arty band is playing for free at wee **Whistler** (p99).

Need to Know

For more information, see Survival Guide (p145)

Currency
US dollar ($)

Language
English

Visas
Visitors from Canada, the UK, Australia, New Zealand and many EU countries do not need a visa for stays of less than 90 days. Other visitors might (see http://travel.state.gov).

Money
ATMs widely available. Credit cards accepted at most hotels, restaurants and shops.

Cell Phones
Europe and Asia GSM 900/1800 standard does not work in the USA. Consider buying a cheap local phone with a pay-as-you-go plan

Time
Central Standard Time (GMT/UTC minus six hours).

Plugs & Adaptors
Plugs have two vertical pins; electrical current is 120V. European visitors will require an adaptor and maybe a transformer.

Tipping
Expected at most places. Restaurant servers: 15% to 20%. Bartenders: 15% per round (minimum per drink $1). Porters: $2 per bag. Hotel maids: $2 to $5 per night. Taxi drivers: 10% to 15%.

① Before You Go

Your Daily Budget

Budget less than $100
- Dorm bed: $35–40
- Lunchtime specials: $10–15
- Discount theater or blues club ticket: $10–25

Midrange $100–300
- Hotel or B&B double room: $150–250
- Dinner in a casual restaurant: $20–30
- Cubs bleacher seat: $40–60

Top End more than $300
- Luxury hotel double room: $400
- Dinner at Alinea: $265
- Lyric Opera ticket: $200

Useful Websites

- **Lonely Planet** (www.lonelyplanet.com/usa/chicago) Bookings, travel forum and photos.
- **Choose Chicago** (www.choosechicago.com) Official tourism site.
- **Chicagoist** (www.chicagoist.com) Quirky take on food, arts and events.
- **Gapers Block** (www.gapersblock.com) News and events site with Chicago attitude.

Advance Planning

Three months before Book your hotel. Reserve at mega-hot restaurants, such as Alinea and Girl and the Goat.

Two weeks before Reserve ahead at your other must-eat restaurants, and book tickets for sports events and museum exhibits.

One week before Check www.hottix.org for half-price theater tickets. Check www.chicagoreader.com to see entertainment options and make bookings.

2 Arriving in Chicago

O'Hare International Airport (ORD; www.
flychicago.com) is 17 miles northwest of
dowtown. Chicago Midway Airport (MDW;
www.flychicago.com) is 11 miles southwest of
downtown. O'Hare is bigger and handles most
of the international flights. Both airports have
easy El train links into the city.

✈ From O'Hare
International Airport

Destination	Best Transport
Loop, South Loop	El train
Near North, Gold Coast	El train, airport shuttle
Lincoln Park	taxi, El train
Lake View & Wrigleyville	taxi, El train
Wicker Park & Bucktown	El train

✈ From Chicago Midway Airport

Destination	Best Transport
Loop, South Loop	El train
Near North, Gold Coast	El train, airport shuttle
Lincoln Park	taxi, El train
Lake View & Wriglelyville	taxi, El train
Wicker Park & Bucktown	El train

From Union Station

All trains and some bus companies arrive at
this huge station in the Loop. Taxis queue
outside the main entrance. The Blue Line
Clinton stop is a few blocks south, but it's not
a good option at night.

3 Getting Around

The public transportation system is a mix
of El trains and buses. Visitors will find the
trains the most useful option. Buy a rechargeable Ventra card at any El station. You must
use the card to enter station turnstiles.

🚆 Train

Chicago's El (it stands for 'elevated,' though
many trains also run underground) is fast,
frequent and will get you to most sights. The
Red and Blue l ines run 24 hours a day; the
six other color-coded lines operate between
4am and 1am. Standard fare is $3 (except
from O'Hare, where it costs $5). A day-pass
costs $10.

🚌 Bus

Buses follow major arterial roads. They operate from early morning until late evening. The
fare is $2.25.

🚲 Bicycle

Lots of locals cycle to get around. Divvy
bikeshare stations are ubiquitous; a day pass
costs $10. Bike rentals for longer rides start
at $18 per two hours.

🚕 Taxi

Cabs are plentiful in the Loop, north to
Andersonville and northwest to Wicker Park/
Bucktown. Flagfall is $3.25, plus $1.80 per
mile and $1 per extra passenger; a 15% tip
is expected. The rideshare company Uber is
also popular in Chicago.

Chicago Neighborhoods

Wrigley Field 👁

Lake View & Wrigleyville (p78)
Baseball lovers and nightlife fans share the bar-filled neighborhood, which parties hard, especially in club-thumping Boystown.

👁 **Top Sights**

Wrigley Field

Lincoln Park & Old Town (p66)
Beaches and zoo animals, top eateries and stylish shops abound in Lincoln Park, while Old Town has Second City comedy.

👁 **Top Sights**

Lincoln Park

Wicker Park, Bucktown & Ukrainian Village (p88)
Few sights, but you can easily spend the day here shopping and the night eating, drinking and hitting the myriad rock clubs.

Near West Side & Pilsen (p100)
Buzzy, top-chef restaurants are the Near West Side's calling card. Mexican taquerias meet hipster hangouts in Pilsen.

Gold Coast (p54)
Furs and Rolls Royces are de rigueur, as are swanky boutiques and cocktail lounges.

⊙ Top Sights

360° Chicago

Museum of Contemporary Art

Near North & Navy Pier (p42)
Shops, restaurants, hotels, galleries, boats and amusements abound in this densely packed quarter.

⊙ Top Sights

Navy Pier

The Loop (p22)
Chicago's center of action for both business and play, with skyscrapers galore.

⊙ Top Sights

Millennium Park

Art Institute of Chicago

Willis Tower

South Loop & Near South Side (p110)
The South Loop bustles with the lakefront Museum Campus. Blues sights and Chinatown are further on.

⊙ Top Sights

Field Museum of Natural History

Lincoln Park

360° Chicago

Museum of Contemporary Art

Navy Pier

Millennium Park

Willis Tower

Art Institute of Chicago

Field Museum of Natural History

Explore
Chicago

Worth a Trip

The Chicago River runs through the city center
PGIAM/GETTY IMAGES ©

Explore

The Loop

The Loop is Chicago's center of action – its financial and historic heart – and it pulsates with energy. Tumultuous tides of pinstriped businessfolk rush the sidewalks, while clattering El trains roar overhead. But it's not all work, work, work here. The Loop is also Chicago's favorite playground. The Art Institute, Willis Tower, Theater District and Millennium Park are top draws among the skyscrapers.

The Sights in a Day

☀ There's lots to see in the Loop. Get an early start at the **Art Institute** (p28), then wander around and explore the neighborhood's art and architecture. **Chicago Cultural Center** (p34) and **Daley Plaza** (p40) are eye poppers.

☀ Grab a quick lunch at **Oasis** (p38) or **Shake Shack** (p38). Active types can rent two-wheelers at **Bike Chicago** (p34) or kayaks from **Urban Kayaks** (p35) and set off on DIY explorations. Late afternoon is usually less crowded for an ascent up **Willis Tower** (p30) to its unnerving glass ledges. Phew. You'll need a drink after that, so it's handy the **Berghoff** (p39) is down the road.

☾ Stop at **Pastoral** (p38) for picnic fixings, then take your spread to **Millennium Park** (p24) for the free evening concert. **Grant Park Orchestra** (p40) zings the strings there three times a week. **Lyric Opera** (p40) and **Goodman Theatre** (p40) are other entertainment options. For dinner, try **Gage** (p36) or **Seven Lions** (p36) for smart gastropub fare.

👁 Top Sights

Millennium Park (p24)

Art Institute of Chicago (p28)

Willis Tower (p30)

❤ Best of Chicago

Architecture

Rookery (p34)

Chicago Cultural Center (p34)

Willis Tower (p30)

Eating

Pizano's (p36)

Native Foods Cafe (p38)

Museums & Galleries

Money Museum (p35)

Art Institute of Chicago (p28)

Sports & Activities

Bike Chicago (p34)

Urban Kayaks (p35)

For Kids

Maggie Daley Park (p34)

Shake Shack (p38)

Getting There

Ⓜ **El** All lines converge in the Loop. Clark/Lake is a useful transfer station between them all. Randolph station is handy for the parks, Quincy station for Willis Tower.

Top Sights
Millennium Park

Chicago's showpiece shines with whimsical public art. Where to start amid the mod designs? Pritzker Pavilion, Frank Gehry's swooping silver band shell? Jaume Plensa's Crown Fountain, with its human gargoyles? Anish Kapoor's silvery sculpture *Cloud Gate* (aka 'the Bean')? Or maybe some place away from the crowds, such as the veiled Lurie Garden abloom with prairie flowers. Summer concerts and winter ice-skating add to the fun.

⊙ Map p32, F2

☎ 312-742-1168

www.millenniumpark.org

201 E Randolph St

admission free

🕔 6am-11pm

Ⓜ Brown, Orange, Green, Purple, Pink Line to Randolph

Frank Gehry's Pritzker Pavilion at Millennium Park

Don't Miss

The Magic Bean

The park's biggest draw is 'the Bean' – officially titled *Cloud Gate* – Anish Kapoor's 110-ton, silver-drop sculpture. It reflects both the sky and the skyline, and everyone clamors around to take a picture and to touch its silvery smoothness. Good vantage points for photos are at the sculpture's north and south ends. For great people-watching, go up the stairs on Washington St, on the Park Grill's north side, where there are shady benches.

Splashy Crown Fountain

Jaume Plensa's Crown Fountain is another crowd-pleaser. Its two, 50ft-high, glass-block towers contain video displays that flash a thousand different faces. The people shown are all native Chicagoans who agreed to strap into Plensa's special dental chair, where he immobilized their heads for filming. Each mug puckers up and spurts water, just like the gargoyles atop Notre Dame Cathedral. A fresh set of nonpuckering faces appears in winter, when the fountain is dry. On hot days the fountain crowds with locals splashing around to cool off. Kids especially love it.

Pritzker Pavilion at Night

Pritzker Pavilion is Millennium Park's acoustically awesome band shell. Architect Frank Gehry designed it and gave it his trademark swooping silver exterior. The pavilion hosts free concerts at 6:30pm most nights June to August. There's indie rock and new music on Monday, world music and jazz on Thursday, and classical music on Wednesday, Friday and Saturday. On Tuesday there's usually a movie beamed onto the huge screen on stage. You can sit up close in the pavilion, or on the grassy Great Lawn that unfurls behind.

☑ Top Tips

▶ The Family Fun Tent in the park's northwest corner offers free arts, crafts and games for kids between 10am and 2pm daily in summer.

▶ Concessions, bathrooms and a gift shop are available at McCormick Tribune Plaza (by the outdoor cafe/ice rink) on Michigan Ave.

▶ Volunteers provide free walking tours of the park at 11:30am and 1pm daily from late May to mid-October. Departure is from the Chicago Cultural Center's visitor center, across the road at 77 E Randolph St.

✗ Take a Break

A burger and creamy caramel milkshake at Shake Shack (p38) provide fuel for more sightseeing. Or go French with a baguette and cafe au lait at Toni Patisserie & Cafe (p39).

Picnic Time

For all shows – but especially the classical ones, which the top-notch Grant Park Orchestra performs – folks bring blankets, picnics, wine and beer. There is nothing quite like sitting on the lawn, looking up through Gehry's wild grid and seeing all the skyscraping architecture that forms the backdrop while hearing the music. If you want a seat up close, arrive early.

Pritzker Pavilion by Day

The pavilion hosts daytime action, too. Concert rehearsals take place Tuesday to Friday, usually from 11am to 1pm, offering a taste of music if you can't catch the evening show. Each Saturday, free exercise classes turn the Great Lawn into a groovy fitness center. Instructors backed by live music-makers lead tai chi at 7am, yoga at 8am, Pilates at 9am and dance at 10am.

The Secret Garden

If the crowds at 'the Bean', Crown Fountain and Pritzker Pavilion are too much, seek out the peaceful Lurie Garden, which uses native plants to form a botanical tribute to Illinois' tall-grass prairie. Visitors often miss the area, because it's hidden behind a big hedge. Yellow coneflowers, poet's daffodils, bluebells and other gorgeous blooms carpet the 5-acre oasis; everything is raised sustainably and without chemicals. A little river runs through it, where folks kick off their shoes and dangle their feet.

BP Bridge & Nichols Bridgeway

In addition to Pritzker Pavilion, Frank Gehry also designed the snaking BP Bridge that spans Columbus Dr. The luminous sheet-metal walkway connects Millennium Park (from the back of the Great Lawn) to Maggie Daley Park, which has ice skating and rock climbing among its activity arsenal. The bridge offers great skyline views, too. The Nichols Bridgeway is another pedestrian-only span. Renzo Piano designed this silver beauty. It arches from the park over Monroe St to the Art Institute's 3rd-floor contemporary sculpture garden (which is free to view). Piano, incidentally, also designed the museum's Modern Wing, which is where the sculpture garden is located.

Cycling & Ice Skating

The McDonald's Cycle Center, in the park's northeast corner near the intersection of Randolph St and Columbus Dr, is the city's main facility for bike commuters, with 300 bike storage spaces plus showers. It's also a convenient place to pick up rental bikes from Bike Chicago, including road, hybrid, tandem and children's bikes. Tucked between 'the Bean' sculpture and the twinkling lights of Michigan Ave, the McCormick Tribune Rink fills with skaters in winter. It operates from late November to late February. Admission is free; skate rental costs $12. In summer the rink morphs into the Park Grill's alfresco cafe.

Ice skaters at Millennium Park

Wrigley Square & Boeing Galleries

The big plaza at the corner of Michigan Ave and Randolph St is Wrigley Sq. The Greek-looking structure rising up from it is the Millennium Monument. It's a replica of the original peristyle that stood here between 1917 and 1953. The semi-circular row of Doric columns shoots up nearly 40ft. It juxtaposes oddly with the modern art throughout the rest of the park, but it's meant to tie past and present together. The lawn in front is dandy for lolling. The two Boeing Galleries flank the park on the north and south sides. The outdoor spaces display changing exhibits of contemporary sculpture and photomurals.

Top Sights
Art Institute of Chicago

The second-largest art museum in the country, the Art Institute houses a treasure trove from around the globe. The collection of impressionist and post-impressionist paintings is second only to those in France, and the number of surrealist works is tremendous. Wander the endless marble and glass corridors, and rooms stuffed with Japanese prints, Grecian urns, suits of armor and one very big, dotted Seurat. The Modern Wing dazzles with Picassos and Mirós.

👁 Map p32, F4

☏ 312-443-3600

111 S Michigan Ave

adult/child $25/free

🕙 10:30am-5pm, to 8pm Thu

Ⓜ Brown, Orange, Green, Purple, Pink Line to Adams

Art Institute of Chicago

Don't Miss

Must-See Works: Floor 2

First up is *A Sunday Afternoon on the Island of La Grande Jatte* by Georges Seurat (Gallery 201). Get close enough for the painting to break down into its component dots and you'll understand why it took Seurat two long years to complete his pointillist masterpiece. Next seek out *Nighthawks* by Edward Hopper (Gallery 262). His lonely, poignant snapshot of four solitary souls at a neon-lit diner was inspired by a Greenwich Ave restaurant in Manhattan. In the next room you'll find *American Gothic* by Grant Wood (Gallery 263). The artist, a lifelong resident of Iowa, used his sister and his dentist as models for the two stern-faced farmers.

Must-See Works: Other Floors

Stop by Marc Chagall's *America Windows* (Gallery 144). He created the huge, blue stained-glass pieces to celebrate the USA's bicentennial. Another favorite is *The Old Guitarist* by Pablo Picasso (Gallery 391). The elongated figure is from the artist's Blue Period. Not far away is Salvador Dalí's *Inventions of the Monsters* (Gallery 396). He painted it in Austria before the Nazi annexation. The title refers to a Nostradamus prediction that the apparition of monsters presages the outbreak of war.

Other Intriguing Sights

The Thorne Miniature Rooms (Lower Level, Gallery 11) and Paperweight Collection (Lower Level, Gallery 15) are awesome, overlooked galleries. The Modern Wing, dazzling with natural light, allows works by Miró, Brancusi and the like to shine and provides gallery space for new, cutting-edge multimedia work.

☑ Top Tips

▶ Allow two hours to browse the museum's highlights; art buffs should allocate much longer.

▶ Advance tickets are available, but unless there's a blockbuster exhibit going on they're usually not necessary. The entrance queue moves fast.

▶ Ask at the information desk about free talks and tours once you're inside.

▶ Download the museum's free app, either at home or using the onsite wi-fi. It offers more than 50 tours through the collection (divided by theme, time available etc).

✖ Take a Break

The cool clubhouse atmosphere at Seven Lions (p36) offers a wine-soaked refuge. The 1898 Berghoff (p39) is tops for a beer and a dose of Chicago history.

Top Sights
Willis Tower

For superlative seekers, Willis Tower is it: Chicago's tallest skyscraper, rising 1450ft into the heavens. Built in 1973 as the Sears Tower, the black-tubed behemoth reigned as the world's tallest building for almost 25 years. It still wins the prize for wildest views from its 103rd-floor Skydeck, where glass-floored ledges jut out in midair and give a knee-buckling perspective smack to the ground. The outward panorama sweeps over four states.

👁 Map p32, A4

📞 312-875-9696

233 S Wacker Dr

adult/child $19.50/12.50

🕙 9am-10pm Apr-Sep, 10am-8pm Oct-Mar

Ⓜ Brown, Orange, Purple, Pink Line to Quincy

Visitors on the Willis Tower Skydeck

Don't Miss

Facts & States

Before ascending, there are factoid-filled murals to ponder and a factoid-filled movie to watch. You'll learn about the 43,000 miles of phone cable used, the 2232 steps to the roof, and how the tower height is the equivalent of 313 Oprahs (or 262 Michael Jordans). Then it's time for the ear-popping, 70-second elevator ride to the top. From here, the entire city stretches below and you can see exactly how Chicago is laid out. On good days you can see for 40 to 50 miles, as far as Indiana, Michigan and Wisconsin. On hazy or stormy days you won't see much at all.

Ledges

The four ledges are on the deck's west side. They're like glass-encased boxes hanging out from the building's frame. If crowds are light, you can sprawl out on one for the ultimate photo op. If the ledges crack – which they did in 2014 when some folks stepped on them – fear not: that's not the glass cracking, but the protective coating covering the 1.5in thick glass. You won't fall. Really. So don't even think about it.

Architecture

Fazlur Khan came up with the design of nine bundled tubes after looking at cigarettes in their pack. The structure lost its 'world's tallest' crown in 1996 to Malaysia's Petronas Twin Towers. It lost its 'USA's tallest' crown in 2013 to New York's One World Trade Center.

☑ Top Tips

▶ Avoid peak times in summer, between 11am and 4pm Friday to Sunday, when queues can surpass an hour.

▶ Buying tickets online saves some time, but there's a $2 surcharge per ticket.

▶ The entrance is on Jackson Blvd, where you go through security. The line to pay is down one level (staff will direct you there).

▶ Ask at the entrance and/or pay desk about visibility. Staff can call the Skydeck and provide updates.

✖ Take a Break

Grab a fat sandwich or red velvet cupcake made by culinary students at **Washburne Cafe** (Map p32, B4; www.washburneculinary. com; 226 W Jackson Blvd; mains $4-6; ⊘7:30am-3:30pm Mon-Fri; Ⓜ Brown, Orange, Purple, Pink Line to Quincy). Global vegan dishes and organic wines feature at Native Foods Cafe (p38).

For reviews see

	Top Sights	p24
	Sights	p34
	Eating	p36
	Drinking	p39
	Entertainment	p40
	Shopping	p41

E

N Wabash Ave

⊗ 14

N Michigan Ave

E Lake St

F

N Stetson Ave

E Randolph St

G

8 ◉

H

Lake Shore East Park

1

⊛ N 0   200 m
     0   0.1 miles

Chicago Cultural Center

Randolph Ⓜ

E Randolph St

McDonald's Cycle Center

E Randolph St

◉ 1

Millennium Chicago Ⓡ

Cultural Center Visitor Center ⓘ

E Washington St

19 ⓟ

McCormick Tribune Ice Rink

Ⓜ Madison

⊗ 15

E Madison St

11   16 ⊗

9 ⊗

Boeing Gallery North

Wrigley Square

AT&T Plaza

Cloud Gate

☆ 25

Jay Pritzker Pavilion

ⓟ
☆ 21

Great Lawn

Boeing Gallery South

Crown Fountain

E Monroe St

◉ 4

Bike Chicago

◉ Millennium Park

Lurie Garden

Nichols Bridgeway

Daley Bicentennial Plaza

Tennis Courts

Tennis Courts

N Columbus Dr

BP Bridge

ⓟ

Tennis Courts

3 Maggie
◉ Daley Park

Maggie Daley Park

Tennis Courts

N Lake Shore Dr

2

3

ⓟ

E Monroe St

20
ⓟ

12 ⊗

Ⓜ E Adams St

Adams

◉ 7

Route 66 Sign ⓟ
23

26 🔒

Art Institute of Chicago ◉

Art Institute of Chicago

E Jackson Blvd

ⓟ

Butler Field

Lakefront Trail

3

S Wabash Ave

Grant Park

S Michigan Ave

Van Buren St (Metra) Ⓡ

S Columbus Dr

Grant Park

Petrillo Music Shell

Lake Michigan

4

E Van Buren St

10
ⓟ

E Congress Pkwy

S Lake Shore Dr

◉ 2

Buckingham Fountain

5

Sights

Chicago Cultural Center
BUILDING

1 💿 Map p32, E2

The block-long building houses terrific art exhibitions and foreign films, as well as jazz, classical and electronic dance music concerts at 12:15pm Monday to Friday. It also contains the world's largest Tiffany stained-glass dome and Chicago's main visitor center. Building tours take place Wednesday, Friday and Saturday at 1:15pm; meet in the Randolph St lobby. And it's all free! (📞312-744-6630; www.chicagoculturalcenter.org; 78 E Washington St; admission free; ⏰9am-7pm Mon-Thu, to 6pm Fri & Sat, 10am-6pm Sun; 🛜; Ⓜ Brown, Orange, Green, Purple, Pink Line to Randolph)

Buckingham Fountain
FOUNTAIN

2 💿 Map p32, G5

Grant Park's centerpiece is one of the world's largest squirters, with a 1.5-million-gallon capacity and a 15-story-high spray. It lets loose on the hour from 9am to 11pm mid-April to mid-October, accompanied at night by multicolored lights and music. (301 S Columbus Dr; Ⓜ Red Line to Harrison)

Maggie Daley Park
PARK

3 💿 Map p32, G2

Families love the park's fanciful free playgrounds in all their enchanted forest and pirate-themed glory. There's also a rock-climbing wall and 18-hole mini-golf course (which becomes an ice-skating ribbon in winter); these features have fees. Multiple picnic tables make the park an excellent spot to relax. It connects to Millennium Park via the pedestrian BP Bridge. (www.maggiedaleypark.com; 337 E Randolph St; admission free; ⏰6am-11pm; 👶; Ⓜ Brown, Orange, Green, Purple, Pink Line to Randolph)

Bike Chicago
CYCLING

4 💿 Map p32, G2

Rent a bike to explore DIY style, or go on a guided tour. The latter cover themes such as lakefront parks and attractions, pizza and hot-dog munching, or downtown's sights and fireworks at night (highly recommended). Prices include lock, helmet and map. This main branch is in Millennium Park; there's a smaller branch on the Riverwalk. (📞312-729-1000; www.bikechicago.com; 239 E Randolph St; per 1/4hr from $9/30; ⏰6:30am-10pm Mon-Fri, from 8am Sat & Sun Jun-Aug, reduced hrs rest of year; Ⓜ Brown, Orange, Green, Purple, Pink Line to Randolph)

Rookery
ARCHITECTURE

5 💿 Map p32, C4

The famed firm of Burnham and Root built the Rookery in 1888. Frank Lloyd Wright remodeled the atrium 19 years later. It's renowned because while it looks hulking and fortresslike outside, it's light and airy inside. You can walk in and look around for free. Tours ($7 to $12) are available at noon

Staircase in the Rookery

weekdays. (www.flwright.org; 209 S LaSalle St; ⏰9:30am-5:30pm Mon-Fri; Ⓜ Brown, Orange, Purple, Plnk Line to Quincy)

Money Museum
MUSEUM

6 Map p32, B4

This small museum in the Federal Reserve Bank of Chicago is fun for a quick browse. The best exhibits include a giant glass cube stuffed with one million $1 bills (it weighs 2000lb) and a counterfeit display differentiating real bills from fakes. Learn why we call $1000 a 'grand', and snap a sweet photo clutching the million-dollar-stuffed briefcase. (📞312-322-2400; www.chicagofed.org; 230 S LaSalle St; admission free; ⏰8:30am-5pm Mon-Fri; Ⓜ Brown, Orange, Purple, Pink Line to Quincy)

Route 66 Sign
HISTORIC SITE

7 ◎ Map p32, E4

Attention Route 66 buffs: the Mother Road's starting point is here. Look for the sign that marks the spot on Adams St's south side as you head west toward Wabash Ave. (E Adams St btwn S Michigan & Wabash Aves; Ⓜ Brown, Orange, Green, Purple, Pink Line to Adams)

Urban Kayaks
KAYAKING

8 ◎ Map p46, H1

Located on the Riverwalk, this outfitter rents kayaks for Chicago River explorations. The company also offers guided tours that glide past downtown's skyscrapers and historic sites. The nighttime fireworks jaunt is a sweet one. Beginners are welcome on tours, but they should take the hour-long introductory class ($45) before paddling on their own. (📞312-965-0035; www.urbankayaks.com; 435 E Riverwalk South; per hr single/tandem $30/50, tours $65-80; ⏲10am-6pm Mon-Fri, from 9am Sat & Sun; Ⓜ Brown, Orange, Green, Purple, Pink Line to State/Lake)

Eating

Gage

MODERN AMERICAN **$$$**

 9 Map p32, E3

This gastropub dishes up fanciful grub, from Gouda-topped venison burgers to mussels vindaloo to Guinness-battered fish and chips. The booze rocks, too, including a solid whiskey list and small-batch beers that pair with the food. (📞312-372-4243; www.thegagechicago.com; 24 S Michigan Ave; mains $17-36; ⏲11am-10pm Mon, to 11pm Tue-Thu, to midnight Fri & Sat, 10am-10pm Sun; Ⓜ Brown, Orange, Green, Purple, Pink Line to Madison)

Cafecito

CUBAN **$**

 10 Map p32, E5

Attached to the HI-Chicago hostel and perfect for the hungry, thrifty traveler, Cafecito serves killer Cuban sandwiches layered with citrus-garlic-marinated roasted pork and ham. Strong coffee and hearty egg sandwiches make a fine breakfast. (📞312-922-2233; www.

cafecitochicago.com; 26 E Congress Pkwy; mains $6-10; ⏲7am-9pm Mon-Fri, 10am-6pm Sat & Sun; 🛜; Ⓜ Brown, Orange, Purple, Pink Line to Library)

Pizano's

PIZZA **$**

 11 Map p32, E3

Pizano's is a good recommendation for deep-dish newbies, since it's not jaw-breakingly thick. The thin-crust pies that hit the checker-clothed tables are good too, winning rave reviews for crispness. Some of the wait staff are characters who've been around forever, which adds to the convivial ambience. It's open late-night (with a full bar), which is a Loop rarity. (📞312-236-1777; www.pizanoschicago.com; 61 E Madison St; 10in pizzas from $14; ⏲11am-2am Sun-Fri, to 3am Sat; 🛜; Ⓜ Brown, Orange, Green, Purple, Pink Line to Madison)

Seven Lions

AMERICAN **$$**

 12 Map p32, E4

Across from the Art Institute, this buzzy but chat-friendly restaurant wafts a meaty menu of crowd pleasers with an inventive edge. Fried chicken skins and pickles and squid-ink spaghetti hit the tables along with fab desserts (mmm, toffee corn puffs) and tremendous wines. Sit indoors in casually elegant, tufted brown leather booths, or outdoors at the hoppin' sidewalk cafe. (📞312-880-0130; www.sevenlionschicago.com; 130 S Michigan Ave; mains $15-27; ⏲11am-11pm Mon-Fri, from 10am Sat & Sun; Ⓜ Brown, Orange, Green, Purple, Pink Line to Adams)

Understand
Chicago Architecture

- -

First Chicago School (1872–99)
Though the 1871 fire didn't seem like an opportunity at the time, it made Chicago what it is today. The chance to reshape the city's burned downtown drew young, ambitious architects including Dankmar Adler, Daniel Burnham, John Root and Louis Sullivan. These men saw the scorched Loop as a sandbox for innovation. Together they made up the First Chicago School (some say they practiced the Commercial style), which stressed economy, simplicity and function. Using steel frames and elevators, their pinnacle achievement was the modern skyscraper, which first popped up in 1885. The Rookery (p34) is a good example of the genre.

Prairie School (1895–1915) & Beaux Arts (1893–1920)
Frank Lloyd Wright, a protégé of Louis Sullivan, endowed Chicago with its most distinctive style, the Prairie School. Wright's designs reflected the Midwest's landscape – low-slung, with long horizontal lines and lots of earth colors. The 1909 Robie House (p123) is his Prairie masterwork.

While the First Chicago School and Prairie School were forward-looking local inventions, beaux arts took after a French fad that stressed antiquity. The popularity of the style was spurred by the colossal French neoclassical structures of Daniel Burnham's 'White City,' built for the 1893 World's Exposition. Beaux arts examples include the Museum of Science & Industry (p123) (a White City remnant) and the Chicago Cultural Center (p34).

Second Chicago School (1946–79) & Skyscrapers Today
Ludwig Mies van der Rohe made sure the city stayed at the forefront of innovation in the 1950s. With his tools of exposed black metal and glass, along with a less-is-more creed, he pioneered the Second Chicago School style of architecture. The Loop's Kluczynski Building (230 S Dearborn St) shows how it's done.

The local architects of Skidmore, Owings & Merrill further developed Mies' ideas, and stretched the modern skyscraper even higher with the John Hancock Center and Sears Tower. The latter remained the world's tallest building for almost a quarter century. Today Chicago continues to push the boundaries of modern design with cloud toppers such as Jeanne Gang's wavy Aqua Tower (225 N Columbus Dr).

Local Life

Riverwalk

The **Riverwalk** (Map p32 E4; Chicago River waterfront along Wacker Dr, btwn N Lake Shore Dr & W Lake St; MBrown, Orange, Green, Purple, Pink, Blue Line to State/Lake) is slowly being developed as a local hangout. Outdoor cafes, wine bars and fountains dot the 1.25-mile-long way on the river's south side. It's a fine spot to escape the crowds and watch boats glide by.

Native Foods Cafe

VEGAN $

13 Map p32, C4

If you're looking for vegan fast-casual fare downtown, Native Foods is your spot. The 'meatball' sandwich rocks the seitan, while the scorpion burger fires up hot-spiced tempeh. Local beers and organic wines accompany the wide-ranging menu. (☑312-332-6332; www. nativefoods.com; 218 S Clark St; mains $9-11; ☉10:30am-9pm Mon-Sat, 11am-7pm Sun; ☑; MBrown, Orange, Purple, Pink Line to Quincy)

Pastoral

DELI $

14 Map p32, E1

Pastoral makes a mean sandwich. Fresh-shaved serrano ham, Basque salami and other carnivorous fixings meet smoky mozzarella, Gruyere and piquant spreads on crusty breads. Vegetarians get a smattering of cheese and veggie options. The shops sells beer and wine, too. There's limited seating, as most folks take away

(especially for picnics in nearby Millennium Park). (☑312-658-1250; www. pastoralartisan.com; 53 E Lake St; sandwiches $8-10; ☉10:30am-8pm Mon-Fri, 11am-6pm Sat & Sun; MBrown, Orange, Green, Purple, Pink Line to Randolph or State/Lake)

Oasis

MIDDLE EASTERN $

15 Map p32, E2

Walk past diamonds, gold and other bling in the jewelers' mall before striking it rich in this cafe at the back. Creamy hummus, crisp falafel and other Middle Eastern favorites fill plates at bargain prices. (☑312-443-9534; 21 N Wabash Ave; mains $5-9; ☉10am-5:30pm Mon-Fri, 11am-4pm Sat; MBrown, Orange, Green, Purple, Pink Line to Madison)

Shake Shack

BURGERS $

16 Map p32, E3

The NYC chain has come to Chicago. The burger spot is beloved for its well-griddled patties under a sweet-and-tangy Shake Sauce, crinkle-cut fries and milkshakes made with creamy custard (and local doughnuts and pie blended in). Are the shakes really the nation's best? The endless crowd of happy slurpers provides the answer. (☑312-646-6005; www.shakeshack.com; 12 S Michigan Ave; mains $5-10; ☉11am-11pm; MBrown, Orange, Green, Purple, Pink Line to Madison)

Drinking

Berghoff
BAR

17 Map p32, D4

The Berghoff was the first spot in town to serve a legal drink after Prohibition (ask to see the liquor license stamped '#1'). Little has changed around the antique wood bar since then. Belly up for frosty mugs of the house-brand beer and order sauerbraten, schnitzel and other old-world classics from the adjoining German restaurant. (www.theberghoff.com; 17 W Adams St; ⊘11am-9pm Mon-Sat; Ⓜ Blue, Red Line to Jackson)

Monk's Pub
PUB

18 Map p32, B1

Grab the brass handles on the huge wooden doors and enter a dimly lit Belgian beer cave. Old barrels, vintage taps and faux antiquarian books set the mood, accompanied by a whopping international brew selection and free, throw-your-shells-on-the-floor peanuts. Office workers and the occasional TV weatherman are the main folks hanging out at Monk's, which also serves good, burger-y pub grub. (www.monkspubchicago.com; 205 W Lake St; ⊘9am-11pm Mon-Fri, 11am-5pm Sat; Ⓜ Blue, Brown, Orange, Green, Purple, Pink Line to Clark/Lake)

Toni Patisserie & Cafe
CAFE

19 Map p32, E2

Toni's provides a cute refuge for a glass of wine. The Parisian-style cafe has a small list of French reds, whites and sparkling wines to sip at the close-set tables while you try to resist the eclairs, macaroons and tiered cakes tempting from the glass case. It also sells bottles for take-out (handy for Millennium Park picnics). (www.tonipatisserie.com; 65 E Washington St; ⊘8am-8pm Mon-Sat, to 5pm Sun; Ⓜ Brown, Orange, Green, Purple, Pink Line to Randolph or Madison)

Miller's Pub
PUB

20 Map p32, E3

The beauty of Miller's isn't so much literal, though it's attractive enough with dark-wood furnishings, stained glass and nostalgic sports photos adorning the walls. The real beauty comes from the late-night hours in an area where most places close by 10pm. Even better: Miller's pours a whopping selection of craft and Belgian brews and serves a big, meaty menu. (www.millerspub.com; 134 S Wabash Ave; ⊘10am-4am; Ⓜ Brown, Orange, Green, Purple, Pink Line to Adams)

 Top Tip

Pack a Picnic

Pack a picnic and meander over to Millennium Park to hear a free concert. Indie rock, jazz or classical performers take the stage nightly, including many big-name musicians. Pastoral (p38) and Toni Patisserie (p39) can set you up with deli goods and wine.

Entertainment

Grant Park Orchestra
CLASSICAL MUSIC

21 ⭐ Map p32, F2

It's a summertime must-do. The Grant Park Orchestra – composed of top-notch musicians from symphonies worldwide – puts on free classical concerts at Millennium Park's Pritzker Pavilion. Patrons bring lawn chairs, blankets, wine and picnic fixings to set the scene as the sun dips, the skyscraper lights flicker on and glorious music fills the night air. (☏312-742-7638; www.grantparkmusicfestival.com; Pritzker Pavilion, Millennium Park; admission free; ⏲6:30pm Wed & Fri, 7:30pm Sat mid-Jun–mid-Aug; Ⓜ Brown, Orange, Green, Purple, Pink Line to Randolph)

🔍 Local Life
Daley Plaza

The eye-popping Picasso sculpture marks the heart of **Daley Plaza** (Map p32, C2; 50 W Washington St; Ⓜ Blue Line to Washington). It's the place to come at lunchtime, particularly when the weather warms. You never know what will be going on – dance performances, bands, ethnic festivals, a farmers market (7am to 3pm Thursdays) – but you do know it'll be free.

Goodman Theatre
THEATER

22 ⭐ Map p32, D1

The Goodman is one of Chicago's premier drama houses, and its Theater District facility is gorgeous. It specializes in new and classic American productions and has been cited several times as one of the best regional theaters in the USA. At 10am, Goodman puts unsold tickets for the current day's performance on sale for half-price online. (☏312-443-3800; www.goodmantheatre.org; 170 N Dearborn St; Ⓜ Brown, Orange, Green, Purple, Pink, Blue Line to Clark/Lake)

Chicago Symphony Orchestra
CLASSICAL MUSIC

23 ⭐ Map p32, E4

Riccardo Muti leads the CSO, one of America's best symphonies, known for fervent subscribers and an untouchable brass section. Cellist Yo-Yo Ma is the group's creative consultant and a frequent soloist. The season runs from September to May at Symphony Center; Daniel Burnham designed the Orchestra Hall. (☏312-294-3000; www.cso.org; 220 S Michigan Ave; Ⓜ Brown, Orange, Green, Purple, Pink Line to Adams)

Lyric Opera Of Chicago
OPERA

24 ⭐ Map p32, A2

Tickets are hard to come by for this bold modern opera company, which fills the chandeliered Civic Opera House with a shrewd mix of common classics and daring premieres from September to March. If your Italian isn't up to snuff, don't be put off; much to the horror of purists, the company projects English 'supertitles' above the proscenium. (☎312-332-2244; www.lyricopera.org; 20 N Wacker Dr; Ⓜ Brown, Orange, Purple, Pink Line to Washington)

Hubbard Street Dance Chicago
DANCE

25 ⭐ Map p32, F2

It is Chicago's preeminent dance company, with a well-deserved international reputation to match. The group is known for energetic and technically virtuoso performances. It leaps at the Harris Theater for Music and Dance in Millennium Park. (☎312-850-9744; www.hubbardstreetdance.com; 205 E Randolph St; Ⓜ Brown, Orange, Green, Purple, Pink Line to Randolph)

Shopping

Chicago Architecture Foundation Shop
SOUVENIRS

26 🏛 Map p32, C4

Skyline posters, Frank Lloyd Wright note cards, skyscraper models and heaps of books celebrate local architecture at this haven for anyone

Top Tip

Photo Op

What's more perfect for your Chicago selfie backdrop than a six-story-high sign spelling the city's name in bright, glittering lights? The eye-popper in front of the 1920s **Chicago Theatre** (www.thechicagotheatre.com; 175 N State St; Ⓜ Brown, Orange, Green, Purple, Pink Line to State/Lake) is an official landmark and sets the scene perfectly.

with an edifice complex. The items make excellent only-in-Chicago-type souvenirs. (www.architecture.org/shop; 224 S Michigan Ave; ⊙9am-6:30pm; Ⓜ Brown, Orange, Green, Purple, Pink Line to Adams)

Optimo Hats
ACCESSORIES

27 🏛 Map p32, D4

Optimo is a Chicago institution, the last custom hat-maker for men in town. Want a lid like Capone? Get one here, made with serious, old-school craftsmanship. Clients include Johnny Depp, Jack White and a slew of local bluesmen. The shop is located in the groovy 1891 Monadnock Building. (www.optimo.com; 320 S Dearborn St; ⊙10am-5pm Mon-Sat; Ⓜ Blue Line to Jackson)

Explore

Near North & Navy Pier

The Near North packs in deep-dish pizza parlors, buzzy bistros, art galleries and so many upscale stores that its main vein – Michigan Ave – has been dubbed the 'Magnificent Mile.' Jutting out to the east is Navy Pier, a cavalcade of kid-oriented shops, rides, attractions and a big freakin' Ferris wheel. Both areas bustle day and night.

The Sights in a Day

☀ Have breakfast at **Xoco** (p49), gobbling the rich churros and chili-spiked hot chocolate. Walk along the **Magnificent Mile** (p48) and ogle the architecture of the **Tribune Tower** (pictured left, p48) and **Wrigley Building** (p48) in between shopping stops. Resistance is futile: give in to the heavenly smell and buy a bag of **Garrett Popcorn** (p52).

☼ Make your way east to **Navy Pier** (p44). Don't be a sissy: get up in the Ferris wheel for killer views of the city. Or rent a bike from **Bobby's Bike Hike** (p48) and head out on the Lakefront Trail. After all the exercise, you've earned a happy-hour drink at **Clark Street Ale House** (p51) or **Henry's Swing Club** (p51).

☾ Sup on swine and wine with the crowds at **Purple Pig** (p49) or fork into sustainable fare with a river view at **Kitchen Chicago** (p50). Later, jazz fans can settle in at **Andy's** (p51), while blues fans can do the same at **Blue Chicago** (p52).

👁 Top Sights

Navy Pier (p44)

♥ Best of Chicago

Architecture
Tribune Tower (p48)

Marina City (p48)

Driehaus Museum (p48)

Eating
Xoco (p49)

Giordano's (p50)

Sports & Activities
Bobby's Bike Hike (p48)

For Kids
Chicago Children's Museum (p49)

Navy Pier (p44)

Shopping
Garrett Popcorn (p52)

Jazz Record Mart (p52)

Getting There

M **El** Red Line to Grand for the Magnificent Mile's south end; Red Line to Chicago for the Mag Mile's north end; Brown, Purple Line to Chicago for River North.

Top Sights
Navy Pier

Navy Pier was once the city's municipal wharf.
Today it's Chicago's most-visited attraction,
with eight million people per year flooding its
half-mile length. Locals may groan about its
commercialization, but even they can't refute
the brilliant lakefront views, cool breezes
and whopping fireworks displays in summer.
Kids go gaga over the high-tech rides, fast-food
restaurants and trinket vendors. Get ready for an
in-your-face carnival experience.

👁 Map p46, H3

600 E Grand Ave

admission free

🕐 10am-10pm Sun-Thu, to
midnight Fri & Sat Jun-Aug,
10am-8pm Sun-Thu, to 10pm
Fri & Sat Sep-May

Ⓜ Red Line to Grand, then
trolley

Navy Pier carousel

Don't Miss

Ferris Wheel & Other Rides

No visit to the pier is complete without a stomach-curdling ride on the gigantic Ferris wheel (recently pumped up from 150ft to 196ft), which unfurls great views. The carousel is a beloved kiddie classic, with bobbing carved horses and organ music. There's also an 18-hole mini-golf course that weaves around the rides. Each attraction costs $6 to $8. For young ones in need of further amusements, the Chicago Children's Museum is on the pier near the main entrance.

Theaters & Tour Boats

Music and theater acts appear throughout the summer at the Skyline Stage, a 1500-seat rooftop venue with a glistening white canopy. An IMAX Theater and the Chicago Shakespeare Theater also call the pier home. Competing tour boats depart from the pier's south side, where you can set sail in everything from a tall-masted schooner to thrill-ride speedboat.

Past & Future

Navy Pier opened in 1916. During the past century it has seen action as a busy inland port, a WWII Navy pilot training center, a university campus, a convention center and now, an entertainment complex. It has had a reputation in recent years as being cheesy, but the city is trying to change that. A multimillion renovation is bringing an ice rink, upgraded eating and drinking options, and more in 2016 and 2017.

☑ Top Tips

▶ A free trolley runs from the Red Line Grand station (the nearest El stop) to Navy Pier from late May to early September. Otherwise it's about a mile-long walk.

▶ Crowds amass for the summer fireworks shows on Wednesdays at 9:30pm and Saturdays at 10:15pm.

▶ In summer the Shoreline water taxi (adult/child $8/4) glides from Navy Pier to the Museum Campus, offering a fun alternative to land-based transport.

✕ Take a Break

Heft a gargantuan slice of stuffed pizza at the pier outpost of Giordano's (p50). Or have a beer and check out the sports memorabilia at **Harry Caray's Tavern** (www.harrycaraystavern. com; 700 E Grand Ave; ⊙11am-10pm Sun-Thu, to midnight Fri & Sat; Ⓜ Red Line to Grand, then trolley), also on the pier.

A

B Washington Square

C **GOLD COAST**

D John Hancock Center

Water Tower Place

W Locust St

W Delaware Pl

W Delaware Pl

E Delaware Pl

W Chestnut St

W Tooker Pl

E Chestnut St

W Chestnut St

W Institute Pl

N Rush St

Chicago

Chicago

E Chicago Ave

W Chicago Ave 15

10

RIVER NORTH GALLERY DISTRICT

NEAR NORTH

W Superior St

N Franklin St

W Huron St

N Clark St

N Dearborn St

N State St

Driehaus Museum

6

14

W Erie St

Magnificent Mile

1

W Ontario St

N Wells St

N LaSalle St

N Wabash Ave

N Michigan Ave (Magnificent Mile)

N St Clair St

20

W Ohio St

13

W Grand Ave

18

Grand

9

W Illinois St

E Illinois St

8

16

12

W Hubbard St

19

E Hubbard St

3

17

Tribune Tower

E Kinzie St

Wrigley Building

W Kinzie St

N Orleans St

Chicago Water Taxi, LaSalle St Stop 11

Marina City

4

Trump Tower

Merchandise Mart

ILLINOIS CENTER

W Wacker Dr

E Wacker Pl

N Wacker Dr

N Franklin St

N Wells St

N LaSalle St

Clark

W Lake St

Clark

State

Lake

N State St

N Wabash Ave

N Garland Ct

N Michigan Ave

N Stetson Ave

Penton Pl

N Mies van der Rohe Way
N Dewitt Pl
E Pearson St
N Lake Shore Dr
Lakefront Trail

Seneca
Park
Lake Shore Park

E Superior St
Northwestern
University Chicago
Campus
N Lake Shore Dr

E Huron St
N Fairbanks Ct

E Erie St

Ohio
Street
Beach

Water
Filtration
Plant

Olive
Park

E Ontario St
N McClurg Ct

STREETERVILLE
E Ohio St

Bobby's
Bike Hike
5

**NAVY
PIER**

E Grand Ave

Chicago
Children's
Museum

E Illinois St
N New St
N McClurg Ct

Navy
Pier

7

City
Front
Plaza

Ogden
Plaza

Shoreline
Water Taxi to
Willis Tower

Shoreline Water Taxi
to Museum Campus

E North Water St

Sheraton Chicago
Hotel and Towers

River
Esplanade

Chicago
River

Hyatt
Regency
Chicago

E Wacker Dr

Urban
Kayaks

N Columbus Dr

Harbor

N Lake Shore Dr

Lakefront Trail

Lake
Michigan

Lake Shore
East Park

Lake Shore
East Park

0   400 m
0   0.2 miles

Sights

Magnificent Mile
STREET

1 ◎ Map p46, D3

Spanning Michigan Ave between the river and Oak St, the Mag Mile is Chicago's much-touted upscale shopping strip, where Bloomingdale's, Apple, Burberry and many more will lighten your wallet. The retailers are mostly high-end chains that have stores nationwide. (www.themagnificentmile.com; N Michigan Ave; Ⓜ Red Line to Grand)

Tribune Tower
ARCHITECTURE

2 ◎ Map p46, D4

Colonel Robert McCormick, eccentric owner of the *Chicago Tribune* in the early 1900s, collected – and asked his reporters to send – rocks from famous buildings and monuments around the world. He stockpiled pieces of the Taj Mahal, Westminster Abbey, the Great Pyramid and 140 or so others, which are now embedded around the tower's base. (435 N Michigan Ave; Ⓜ Red Line to Grand)

Wrigley Building
ARCHITECTURE

3 ◎ Map p46, D4

The Wrigley Building glows as white as the Doublemint Twins' teeth, day or night. Chewing-gum guy William Wrigley built it that way on purpose, because he wanted it to be attention-grabbing like a billboard. More than 250,000 glazed terra-cotta tiles make up the facade; a computer database tracks each one and indicates when each needs to be cleaned and polished. (400 N Michigan Ave; Ⓜ Red Line to Grand)

Marina City
ARCHITECTURE

4 ◎ Map p46, C4

For postmodern fun, check out the twin corncob towers of the 1964 Marina City. Bertrand Goldberg designed the futuristic high-rise, and it has become an iconic part of the Chicago skyline (check out the cover of the Wilco CD *Yankee Hotel Foxtrot*). And yes, there is a marina at the towers' base. (300 N State St; Ⓜ Brown, Orange, Green, Purple, Pink Line to State/Lake)

Bobby's Bike Hike
CYCLING

5 ◎ Map p46, G3

Locally based Bobby's earns rave reviews from riders. It rents bikes and has easy access to the Lakefront Trail. It also offers cool tours ($35 to $59) of South Side gangster sites, the lakefront, nighttime vistas and venues to indulge in pizza and beer. The Tike Hike caters to kids. Enter through the covered driveway to reach the shop. (📞 312 245-9300; www.bobbysbikehike.com; 540 N Lake Shore Dr; per 2/4hr from $20/25; ⏰ 8:30am-8pm Mon-Fri, from 8am Sat & Sun Jun-Aug, 9am-7pm Sep-Nov & Mar-May; Ⓜ Red Line to Grand)

Driehaus Museum
MUSEUM

6 ◎ Map p46, C2

Set in the exquisite Nickerson Mansion, the Driehaus immerses visitors in Gilded Age decorative arts and architecture. You'll feel like a *Great Gatsby* character as you wander three floors stuffed with sumptuous *objets* and stained glass. Recommended guided tours ($5 extra) are available four times daily. The price seems steep, but the museum is a prize for those intrigued by opulent interiors. (☑312-482-8933; www.driehausmuseum.org; 40 E Erie St; adult/child $20/10; ☉10am-5pm Tue-Sun; Ⓜ Red Line to Chicago)

Chicago Children's Museum
MUSEUM

7 ◉ Map p46, H3

Designed to challenge the imaginations of toddlers to 10-year-olds, this colorful museum near Navy Pier's main entrance gives young visitors enough hands-on exhibits to keep them climbing and creating for hours. Among the favorites, Dinosaur Expedition explores the world of paleontology and lets kids excavate 'bones.' They can also climb a ropey schooner and bowl in a faux alley. (☑312-527-1000; www.chicagochildrensmuseum.org; 700 E Grand Ave; admission $14; ☉10am-5pm Mon-Wed, to 8pm Thu, to 6pm Fri, to 7pm Sat & Sun; ⬥; Ⓜ Red Line to Grand, then trolley)

Eating

Xoco
MEXICAN $

8 ✕ Map p46, B4

Crunch into warm churros with chili-spiked hot chocolate for breakfast,

Wrigley Building (front) and Trump Tower

meaty *tortas* (sandwiches) for lunch and rich *caldos* (soups) for dinner at celeb chef Rick Bayless' Mexican street-food joint. His upscale restaurants Frontera Grill and Topolobampo are next door, but you'll need reservations or a whole lot of patience to get in. FYI, it's pronounced 'SHOW-co'. (www.rickbayless.com; 449 N Clark St; mains $10-14, ☉8am-9pm Tue-Thu, to 10pm Fri & Sat; Ⓜ Red Line to Grand)

Purple Pig
MEDITERRANEAN $$

9 ✕ Map p46, D3

The Pig's Magnificent Mile location, wide-ranging meat and veggie menu and late-night serving hours make it a crowd pleaser. Milk-braised pork shoulder is the hamtastic specialty. Dishes are meant to be shared, and the long list of affordable vinos gets the good times rolling at communal tables both indoors and out. No reservations. (☑312-464-1744; www.thepurplepigchicago.com; 500 N Michigan Ave; small plates $9-19; ⏱11:30am-midnight Sun-Thu, to 1am Fri & Sat; ✍; MRed Line to Grand)

Giordano's

PIZZA $$

 10 Map p46, D2

Giordano's makes 'stuffed' pizza, a bigger, doughier version of deep dish.

 Local Life
River North Galleries

When local loft owners need fine art for their walls, they head to River North's gallery district. You can see several venues within a few-blocks. Franklin and Superior Sts are the bulls-eye. Most galleries have maps you can take which cover the scene. Local favorites include **Richard Norton Gallery** (Map p46, A4; www.richardnortongallery.com; 222 Merchandise Mart Plaza; ⏱9am-5pm Mon-Fri; MBrown, Purple Line to Merchandise Mart), which specializes in impressionist, Modernist and historic Chicago-focused works. **Project Room** (Map p46, A2; www.theprojectroompb.com; 217 W Huron St ; ⏱noon-6pm Wed-Sat; MBrown, Purple Line to Chicago) organizes globe-spanning exhibits such as Tibetan photos, Cuban prints and Chilean paintings.

It's awesome. If you want a slice of heaven, order the 'special', a stuffed pie containing sausage, mushroom, green pepper and onions. (☑312-951-0747; www.giordanos.com; 730 N Rush St; small pizzas from $15.50; ⏱11am-11pm Sun-Thu, to midnight Fri & Sat; MRed Line to Chicago)

Kitchen Chicago

MODERN AMERICAN $$

 11 Map p46, B4

The space right on the river is a knock-out: an airy room of exposed concrete, glittery chandeliers and chunky wood tables with water views. The motto is 'community through food,' which translates into an upscale hippie-type ambiance where you can watch the chefs create your sustainably sourced fava bean bruschetta, lemon-sauced chicken and smoked mussels in the open kitchen. (☑312-836-1300; www.thekitchen.com; 316 N Clark St; mains $18-34; ⏱11am-10pm; MBlue, Brown, Orange, Green, Purple, Pink Line to Clark/Lake)

Billy Goat Tavern

BURGERS $

 12 Map p46, D4

Tribune and *Sun-Times* reporters have guzzled in the subterranean Billy Goat for decades. Order a 'cheezborger' and Schlitz beer, then look around at the newspapered walls to get the scoop on infamous local stories, such as the Cubs Curse. The place is a tourist magnet, but a deserving one. Follow the tavern signs that lead below Michigan Ave to get here. (☑312-222-1525; www.billygoattavern.com; lower level, 430 N

Michigan Ave; burgers $4-6; ⏱6am-2am Mon-Fri, 10am-2am Sat & Sun; Ⓜ Red Line to Grand)

Eataly
ITALIAN $$

13 Map p46, C3

This two-story food emporium overwhelms when you step inside. The winners among the many restaurants and cafe counters strewn throughout include La Focaccia (warm, bread-y goodness), Nutella (spread thick on bread or in crepes) and the Birreria (suds brewed onsite). Can't decide? Hit the wine bar (2nd floor) for a takeaway glass, then sip as you wander the premises to choose. (☏312-521-8700; www.eataly.com; 43 E Ohio St; items $3-13, mains $14-25; ⏱11am-10pm; Ⓜ Red Line to Grand)

Mr Beef
SANDWICHES $

14 Map p46, A2

It's a classic for the local Italian beef sandwich specialty. The signature item arrives on a long, spongy white bun that begins dribbling (that's a good thing!) after a load of the spicy meat and cooking juices has been ladled on. The *giardiniera* (spicy pickled vegetables) adds heat. Don't be afraid of the dumpy decor. Cash only. (☏312-337-8500; 666 N Orleans St; sandwiches $6-9; ⏱9am-5pm Mon-Fri, 10am-3pm Sat, plus 10:30pm-4am Fri & Sat; Ⓜ Brown, Purple Line to Chicago)

Drinking

Clark Street Ale House
BAR

15 Map p46, B2

Do as the retro sign advises and 'Stop & Drink Liquor.' Midwestern microbrews are the main draw. Work up a thirst on the free pretzels, order a three-beer sampler for $7 and cool off in the beer garden out back. (www.clarkstreetalehouse.com; 742 N Clark St; ⏱4pm-4am Mon-Fri, from 11am Sat & Sun; Ⓜ Red Line to Chicago)

Henry's Swing Club
BAR

16 Map p46, C4

Many bars in this neighborhood are annoyingly trendy and uppity. Henry's is so refreshing because it's the opposite: welcoming, laid-back and relatively cheap. Hang out on one of the couches, play pool or cards, swill a craft cocktail or small-batch beer (six on tap, but many more by the bottle). Henry's serves its famed sliders (aka mini-burgers) until late night. (www.henrys-swing-club.com; 18 W Hubbard St; ⏱5pm-2am Sun & Tue-Thu, 3pm-2am Fri, 5pm-3am Sat; Ⓜ Red Line to Grand)

Entertainment

Andy's
JAZZ

17 Map p46, C4

This comfy jazz club programs a far-ranging lineup of local traditional, swing, bop, Latin, fusion and Afro-pop

Local Life

Green Door Tavern

The **Green Door** (☏312-664-5496; www.greendoorchicago.com; 678 N Orleans St; mains $10-14; ☺11:30am-2am Mon-Fri, from 10am Sat & Sun; Ⓜ Brown, Purple Line to Chicago), tucked in an 1872 building, is your place to mingle with locals over beers and well-made burgers amid old photos and memorabilia. During Prohibition, a door painted green meant there was a speakeasy in the basement. It's now a cocktail bar.

acts, along with the occasional big-name performer. It has been on the scene for several years and its downtown location makes it a popular spot for postwork boppers. (www.andysjazzclub.com; 11 E Hubbard St; cover charge $10-15; ☺4pm-1:30am; Ⓜ Red Line to Grand)

Blue Chicago   BLUES

18 ⭐ Map p46, B3

If you're staying in the neighborhood and don't feel like hitting the road, you won't go wrong at this friendly mainstream blues club. Commanding local acts wither the mics nightly. (☏312-661-0100; www.bluechicago.com; 536 N Clark St; cover charge $10-12; ☺8pm-2am Sun-Fri, to 3am Sat; Ⓜ Red Line to Grand)

Shopping

Jazz Record Mart   MUSIC

19 🔒 Map p46, C4

You have to hunt for this place, but jazzheads, blues aficionados and vintage vinyl collectors seek it out, as it makes the short list of best record stores in the nation. You can spend hours fingering through the rows of dusty LPs or chatting with the dedicated staff about local blues and jazz. (www.jazzmart.com; 27 E Illinois St; ☺10am-7pm Mon-Sat, 11am-5pm Sun; Ⓜ Red Line to Grand)

Garrett Popcorn   FOOD

20 🔒 Map p46, D3

Like lemmings drawn to a cliff, people form long lines outside this store on the Mag Mile. Granted, the caramel corn is heavenly and the cheese popcorn decadent, but is it worth waiting in the whipping snow for a chance to buy some? Actually, it is. Buy the Chicago Mix, which combines the two flavors. Enter from Ontario St. (☏312-944-2630; www.garrettpopcorn.com; 625 N Michigan Ave; ☺10am-8pm Mon-Thu, to 10pm Fri & Sat, to 7pm Sun; Ⓜ Red Line to Grand)

Understand

Al Capone

Early Days

Alphonse Gabriel Capone was born in New York City in 1899. He moved to Chicago 20 years later, encouraged by his gangster mentor Johnny Torrio, who promised a city of opportunity. Capone quickly moved up the local ranks and became the mob boss in 1924, taking control of the city's South Side and expanding his empire by making 'hits' on his rivals. Capone typically sent his submachine-gun-toting lieutenants to carry out these bloody acts. Incidentally, Capone earned the nickname 'Scarface' after a dance-hall fight left him with a large scar on his left cheek.

Success & Downfall

Prohibition fueled the success of the Chicago mob. Not surprisingly, the citizens' thirst for booze wasn't eliminated by government mandate, and gangs made fortunes dealing in illegal beer, gin and other intoxicants. Commenting on the hypocrisy of a society that would ban booze and then pay him a fortune to sell it, Capone said: 'When I sell liquor, they call it bootlegging. When my patrons serve it on silver trays on Lake Shore Dr, they call it hospitality.' Capone remained the mob boss from 1924 to 1931, until Eliot Ness brought him down on tax evasion charges. Ness was the federal agent whose task force earned the name 'The Untouchables' because its members were supposedly impervious to bribes. Capone served his jail sentence from 1932 to 1939. By the time he left, he was disabled by syphilis.

Sites to See

Infamous Capone sites to see include **Holy Name Cathedral** (735 N State St, Near North), where Capone ordered a couple of hits that took place near the church. You'll have to use your imagination for the **St Valentine's Day Massacre Site** (2122 N Clark St, Lincoln Park), where Capone's thugs killed seven members of Bugs Moran's gang. The area is now a parking lot. The Green Mill (p87) was Capone's favorite speakeasy. The gangster is buried in Mt Carmel Cemetery in suburban Hillside. His simple gravestone reads, 'Alphonse Capone, 1899–1947, My Jesus Mercy.'

Explore

Gold Coast

The Gold Coast has been the address of Chicago's wealthiest residents for more than 125 years. Bejeweled women glide in and out of the neighborhood's stylish boutiques. The occasional Rolls Royce wheels along the leafy streets. The cloud-poking 360° Chicago and provocative Museum of Contemporary Art are the top attention grabbers. At night, Rush St entertains with swanky steakhouses and piano lounges.

The Sights in a Day

☀ Breakfast at **Hendrickx Belgian Bread Crafter** (p64) is a sweet affair. Afterward take a stroll on **Oak Street Beach** (p62), then see what head-scratching exhibits are on at the **Museum of Contemporary Art** (p58).

☀ Book lovers should check out **Newberry Library** (p62), while fans of antique hemorrhoid surgery kits should peruse the **International Museum of Surgical Science** (p62). If you're at the latter, be sure and walk down nearby Astor St and behold the elegant manors, including Hugh Hefner's **Original Playboy Mansion** (p63).

☾ Nighttime is prime time to take the lickety-split elevator up 94 floors to the **360° Chicago** (p56) observatory. Then again, you could go higher – to the 96th floor – and see the same view from the **Signature Lounge** (p64). For dinner, join the chi chi crowd at **Gibson's** (p64).

👁 **Top Sights**

360° Chicago (p56)

Museum of Contemporary Art (p58)

♥ **Best of Chicago**

Drinking & Nightlife
Signature Lounge (p64)

For Kids
American Girl Place (p65)

Hershey's (p65)

Lego Store (p65)

Sports & Activities
Oak Street Beach (p62)

Eating
Hendrickx Belgian Bread Crafter (p64)

Museums & Galleries
International Museum of Surgical Science (p62)

Museum of Contemporary Art (p58)

Getting There

Ⓜ **El** Red Line to Clark/Division for the neighborhood's northern reaches; Red Line to Chicago for southern areas.

🚌 **Bus** No. 151 runs along Michigan Ave, handy for farther-flung sights.

Top Sights
360° Chicago

360° Chicago – in the John Hancock Center, the city's fourth-tallest skyscraper – is a dandy place to get high. In many ways the view here surpasses the one at Willis Tower, as the Hancock is closer to the lake. The city sparkles out in unfettered vistas to the north, south and west, while Navy Pier bobs to the east. If that's not enough, the observatory offers a couple of lofty thrill features as well.

👁 Map p60, D7

📞 888-875-8439

www.360chicago.com

875 N Michigan Ave

adult/child $19/13

🕙 9am-11pm

Ⓜ Red Line to Chicago

John Hancock Center

Don't Miss

Observatory Lowdown

360° Chicago is the official name of the Hancock Center's 94th-floor observatory. It offers informative displays that tell you the names of the surrounding buildings. It has the 'skywalk,' a sort of screened-in porch that lets you feel the wind and hear the city sounds. The biggest draw is TILT, aka floor-to-ceiling windows that you stand in as they move and tip out over the ground. It costs $7 extra and is actually less spine tingling than it sounds. The observatory is probably your best bet if you have kids or if you're a newbie and want to beef up your Chicago knowledge. But there are other options...

Observatory Alternatives

Not interested in frivolities? Shoot straight up to the 96th-floor Signature Lounge, where the view is free if you buy a drink ($8 to $16). That's right, here you'll get a glass of wine and a comfy seat while staring out at almost identical views from a few floors higher. The elevators for the lounge (and its companion restaurant on the 95th floor) are separate from the observatory. Look for signs that say 'Signature 95th/96th' one floor up from the observatory entrance.

Architecture

The Hancock Center was completed in 1969. Fazlur Khan and Bruce Graham were the chief architects, and they designed the structure to sway 5in to 8in in Chicago's windy conditions. They went on to build the Willis Tower four years later.

JUAN SILVA/GETTY IMAGES ©

☑ Top Tips

▶ Go at night, when the views are particularly awesome. On Wednesday and Saturday evenings in summer there's the bonus of seeing Navy Pier's fireworks.

▶ Feel the speed as you ascend in the elevators. They're moving at 20mph.

▶ If you're short on time, the Hancock observatory is often less crowded than the one at Willis Tower.

✖ Take a Break

Join dapper residents from the neighboring high-rises for a Manhattan at the Coq d'Or (p64) lounge. Hendrickx Belgian Bread Crafter (p64) hits the spot for waffles and other sweet treats.

Top Sights
Museum of Contemporary Art

Consider it the Art Institute's brash, rebellious sibling, with especially strong minimalist, surrealist and conceptual photography collections, and permanent works by René Magritte, Cindy Sherman and Andy Warhol. Covering art from 1945 onward, the MCA's collection spans the gamut, with displays arranged to blur the boundaries between painting, sculpture, video and other media. Exhibits change regularly so you never know what you'll see, but count on it being offbeat and provocative.

⊙ Map p60, D8

www.mcachicago.org

220 E Chicago Ave

adult/student $12/7

🕙 10am-8pm Tue, to 5pm Wed-Sun

Ⓜ Red Line to Chicago

Front entrance of the Museum of Contemporary Art

Don't Miss

Exhibitions

The MCA mounts themed exhibitions that typically focus on underappreciated or up-and-coming artists that curators are introducing to American audiences. For example, you might see a three-decade retrospective of German artist Isa Genzken's sculpture, or Turner Prize–winner Simon Starling's mixed-media works made of recycled materials. Shows last three months or so before the galleries morph into something new.

Sculpture Garden & Front Plaza

The terraced sculpture garden at the back of the museum makes for a nifty browse. In summer a jazz band plays amid the greenery every Tuesday at 5:30pm. Patrons bring blankets and sip drinks from the bar. The museum's front plaza also sees lots of action, especially on Tuesday mornings when a farmers market with veggies, cheeses and baked goods sets up from 7am to 2pm. Both events are big local to-dos.

Arty Theater

The MCA's theater regularly hosts dance, music and film events by contemporary A-listers. Much of it is pretty far out, say an Inuit throat singer performing to a silent film backdrop, or a play about ventriloquists performed by a European puppet troupe, or nude male dancers leaping in a piece about how technology affects life. Bonus: a theater ticket stub provides free museum admission any time during the week after the show.

☑ Top Tips

▶ Docents lead free 45-minute tours through the galleries daily at 1pm, as well as Tuesdays at 2pm, and weekends at 2pm and 3pm. Meet at the 2nd-floor visitor service desk.

▶ Tuesdays are often crowded, as locals can visit for free on that day.

▶ The museum's shop wins big points for its jewelry pieces and colorful children's toys.

✖ Take a Break

The MCA has a cafe onsite that serves sandwiches, salads, beer and wine. It's open the same hours as the museum. The city's most viewtastic bar is a few blocks away at the Signature Lounge (p64), 96 floors up in the Hancock Center.

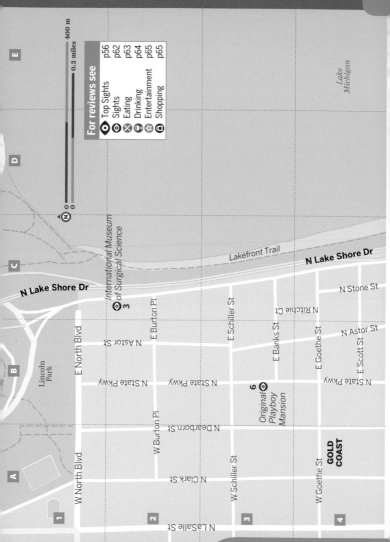

400 m
0.2 miles

For reviews see
◉ Top Sights p56
⊙ Sights p62
✗ Eating p63
🍸 Drinking p64
✪ Entertainment p65
🛍 Shopping p65

Lake Michigan

Lakefront Trail

N Lake Shore Dr

N Lake Shore Dr

International Museum of Surgical Science
◉3

Lincoln Park

N Stone St

N Astor St

E Burton Pl

E Schiller St

N Ritchie Ct

N Astor St

E Banks St

N Goethe St

E Goethe St

N State Pkwy

N State Pkwy

N State Pkwy

N State Pkwy

E Scott St

W Burton Pl

N Dearborn St

Original Playboy Mansion
⊙6

W North Blvd

E North Blvd

W Schiller St

N Clark St

N LaSalle St

W Goethe St

W North Blvd

GOLD COAST

1

2

3

4

N Lake Shore Dr

N Lake Shore Dr

E Division St

E Elm St

E Cedar St

E Bellevue Pl

E Oak St

2 Oak Street Beach

Oak St Beach

E Walton St

E Lake Shore Dr

E Walton St

N Mies van der Rohe Way

N DeWitt Pl

John Hancock Center

10 360°

Chicago

13 Water Tower Place

15

11

N Michigan Ave

Lake Shore Park

Northwestern University Chicago Campus

E Pearson St

Museum of Contemporary Art

Seneca Park

12

E Chicago Ave

E Chestnut St

E Delaware Pl

N Rush St

N Wabash Ave

Water Tower

14

Chicago

E Division St

W Elm St

W Maple St

W Oak St

N Dearborn St

N Clark St

N State St

N Rush St

7

8

Clark/Division

W Division St

W Delaware Pl

Newberry Library **4**

Washington Square

5 Washington Square

W Chestnut St

W Chestnut St

W Chicago Ave

NEAR NORTH

N LaSalle St

5

6

7

8

A

B

C

D

E

Sights

Water Tower
LANDMARK

1 Map p60, C8

The 154ft-tall, turreted tower is a defining city icon: it was the sole downtown survivor of the 1871 Great Chicago Fire, thanks to its yellow limestone bricks that that withstood the flames. Today the tower houses the free City Gallery (open 10am to 6:30pm), showcasing Chicago-themed works by local photographers and artists and well worth a peek. (108 N Michigan Ave; Ⓜ Red Line to Chicago)

Oak Street Beach
BEACH

2 ◉ Map p60, D6

This beach packs in bodies beautiful at the edge of downtown in the shadow of skyscrapers. Lifeguards are on duty in summer. You can rent umbrellas and lounge chairs. The island-y, yellow-umbrella-dotted cafe provides drinks and DJs. (www.cpd-beaches.com; 1000 N Lake Shore Dr; Ⓜ Red Line to Chicago)

International Museum of Surgical Science
MUSEUM

3 ◉ Map p60, C2

Amputation saws, iron lungs and other early tools of the trade are strewn throughout a creaky, Gold Coast mansion. The ancient Roman vaginal speculum leaves a lasting impression, while the pointy-ended hemorrhoid surgery instruments serve as a reminder to eat lots of fiber. The cadaver murals are available as post-cards in the gift shop. (☏312-642-6502; www.imss.org; 1524 N Lake Shore Dr; adult/child $15/7, Tue free; ⊙10am-4pm Tue-Fri, to 5pm Sat & Sun; ☐151)

Newberry Library
LIBRARY

4 ◉ Map p60, A7

The Newberry's public galleries are for bibliophiles: those who swoon over

---

Understand
Astor Street

In the 1880s Chicago's rich and powerful families began moving to Astor St and trying to outdo each other with palatial homes. The mansions rising up in the 1300 to 1500 blocks reflect the grandeur of that heady period. **Cyrus McCormick Mansion** (Map p60, B2; 1500 N Astor St) is a neighborhood standout. New York architect Stanford White designed the 1893 neoclassical beauty, which is now divided into luxury condos. The 1885 **Archbishop's Residence** (Map p60, B1; 1555 N State St) is another eye-popper, complete with 19 chimneys. Alas, the current archbishop does not live on site, though the diocese still owns the building.

original Thomas Paine pamphlets about the French Revolution, or get weak-kneed seeing Thomas Jefferson's copy of the *History of the Expedition under Captains Lewis and Clark* (with margin notes!). Exhibits rotate yellowed manuscripts and tattered first editions from the library's extensive collection. The onsite bookstore is tops for Chicago-themed tomes. (☎312-943-9090; www.newberry.org; 60 W Walton St; admission free; ☉9am-5pm Tue-Sat; Ⓜ Red Line to Chicago)

Washington Square
PARK

5 ◉ Map p60, A7

This plain-looking park across from the Newberry Library has quite a history. In the 1920s it was known as 'Bughouse Square,' where communists, socialists, anarchists and other -ists congregated and gave soapbox orations. (Many supposedly lived in nearby 'bughouses,' or cheap hotels, hence the nickname.) Clarence Darrow and Carl Sandburg are among the respected speakers who climbed up and shouted. (901 N Clark St; Ⓜ Red Line to Chicago)

Original Playboy Mansion
BUILDING

6 ◉ Map p60, B3

The sexual revolution started in the basement 'grotto' of this 1899 manor. Hugh Hefner bought it in 1959 and hung a brass plate over the door warning 'If You Don't Swing, Don't Ring.' In the mid-1970s Hef decamped to LA. The building contains condos

Oak Street Beach

now, but a visit still allows you to boast 'I've been to the Playboy Mansion.' (1340 N State Pkwy; Ⓜ Red Line to Clark/Division)

Eating

Le Colonial
FRENCH, VIETNAMESE $$$

7 ✕ Map p60, B6

Step into the dark-wood, candle-lit room, where ceiling fans swirl lazily and big-leafed palms sway in the breeze, and you'd swear you were in 1920s Saigon. Le Colonial is perfect for a romantic date. Staff can arrange vegetarian and gluten-free substitutions among the curries and banana-leaf-wrapped fish dishes. If you want spicy, be specific; everything typically comes out mild. (📞312-255-0088; www.lecolonialchicago.com; 937 N Rush St; mains $20-29; ⏱11:30am-3pm & 5-11pm Mon-Fri, to midnight Sat, to 10pm Sun; 🍴; Ⓜ Red Line to Chicago)

Gibson's
STEAKHOUSE $$$

8 🍴 Map p60, B6

There is a scene nightly at this local original. Politicians, movers, shakers and the shaken-down swirl the famed martinis and compete for prime table space in the buzzing dining room. The rich and beautiful mingle at the bar. As for the meat on the plates, the steaks are as good as they come and ditto for the ginormous lobsters. (📞312-266-8999; www.gibsonssteakhouse.com; 1028 N Rush St; mains $40-55; ⏱11am-midnight; Ⓜ Red Line to Clark/Division)

Local Life

Hendrickx Belgian Bread Crafter

Hiding in a nondescript apartment building, tiny **Hendrickx Belgian Bread Crafter** (📞312-649-6717; www.hendrickxbakery.com; 100 E Walton St; snacks $3-9; ⏱8am-7pm Tue-Sat, 9am-3pm Sun; Ⓜ Red Line to Chicago) is a local secret. Push open the bright-orange door and behold the waffles, white-chocolate bread and dark-chocolate croissants among the flaky, buttery, Belgian treats.

Tempo Cafe
AMERICAN $

9 🍴 Map p60, B7

Bright and cheery, this diner brings most of its meals to the table the way they're meant to be served – in a skillet. The omelet-centric menu includes all manner of fresh veggies and meat. It's nothing fancy, but it is open round the clock and makes for a relatively cheap meal in the pricey Gold Coast. Cash only. (📞312-943-3929; 6 E Chestnut St; mains $8-15; ⏱24hr; Ⓜ Red Line to Chicago)

Drinking

Signature Lounge
LOUNGE

10 🍸 Map p60, D7

Grab the elevator to the 96th floor of the John Hancock Center and order a beverage while looking out over the city from some 1000ft up in the sky. It's particularly gape-worthy at night. Ladies: don't miss the bathroom view. Note that children aren't allowed in the lounge after 7pm. (www.signature-room.com; 875 N Michigan Ave; ⏱11am-12:30am Sun-Thu, to 1:30am Fri & Sat; Ⓜ Red Line to Chicago)

Coq d'Or
LOUNGE

11 🍸 Map p60, C6

This classy joint in the Drake Hotel opened the day after Prohibition was repealed. It offers a taste of old Chicago – burgundy-colored leather booths, a tuxedoed bartender and bejeweled women in furs sipping Manhattans. A piano player starts

tinkling the ivories around 7pm.
(☏312-787-2200; 140 E Walton St; ⊘11am-
2am Mon-Sat, to 1am Sun; Ⓜ Red Line to
Chicago)

Entertainment

Lookingglass Theatre Company   THEATER

12 Map p60, C8

This well-regarded troupe works in
a nifty theater hewn from the old
Water Works building. The ensemble
cast – which includes cofounder David
Schwimmer of TV's *Friends* – often
uses physical stunts and acrobatics to
enhance its dreamy, magical, literary
productions. (☏312-337-0665; www.
lookingglasstheatre.org; 821 N Michigan Ave;
Ⓜ Red Line to Chicago)

Shopping

American Girl Place   CHILDREN

13 🔒 Map p60, C7

This is not your mother's doll shop; it's
an *experience*. Here, dolls are treated
as real people: the 'hospital' carts them
away in wheelchairs for repairs, and
the cafe seats the dolls as part of the
family during tea service. While there

are American Girl stores in many cities,
this flagship remains the largest and
busiest. (www.americangirl.com; 835 N Michigan
Ave; ⊘10am-8pm Mon-Thu, 9am-9pm Fri &
Sat, 9am-6pm Sun; 🚼; Ⓜ Red Line to Chicago)

Hershey's   FOOD

14 🔒 Map p60, C8

How about a personalized chocolate
bar with your photo on the wrapper?
Hershey's has a handful of flashy retail
stores around the globe and one is right
here on the Mag Mile. Seasonal sweets
and hard-to-find flavors of Kisses and
other chocolates stock the shelves and
there are usually samples to be scoffed.
(www.thehersheycompany.com; 822 N Michigan
Ave; ⊘10am-8pm Sun-Thu, to 10pm Fri & Sat;
📶🚼; Ⓜ Red Line to Chicago)

Lego Store   CHILDREN

15 🔒 Map p60, D8

After ooohing and aahhing at the
cool models of rockets, castles and
dinosaurs scattered throughout the
store, kids can build their own designs
at pint-sized tables equipped with
bins of the signature little bricks. It's
located in Water Tower Place on the
2nd floor. (www.lego.com; 835 N Michigan
Ave; ⊘10am-9pm Mon-Sat, 11am-6pm Sun;
🚼; Ⓜ Red Line to Chicago)

Explore

Lincoln Park & Old Town

Lincoln Park – the green space – is the city's premier playground of lagoons, footpaths, beaches and zoo animals. Lincoln Park – the surrounding neighborhood – adds top-notch restaurants, kicky shops and lively blues and rock clubs to the mix. Next door, stylish Old Town hangs on to its free-spirited past with artsy bars and improv comedy bastion Second City.

The Sights in a Day

🔆 Begin with a wander in **Lincoln Park** (p68). You could spend the whole morning communing with lions, tigers and polar bears at **Lincoln Park Zoo** (p72). For a more tranquil scene, browse the blooms at **Lincoln Park Conservatory** (p72) or meet the butterflies at **Peggy Notebaert Nature Museum** (pictured left; p72).

☀️ Head south for fun in the sun at **North Avenue Beach** (p72). **Chicago History Museum** (p72) is nearby, where you can see the bell from Mrs O'Learay's cow (the bovine that took the rap for starting the 1871 Great Fire). Head into Old Town on Wells St, filled with browsable spots such as **Spice House** (p77) and **La Fournette** (p74).

🌙 If 20 courses of molecular gastronomy sounds good, try to score seats at **Alinea** (p73). If not, make it an evening of improv at **Second City** (p76), followed by drinks at **Old Town Ale House** (p75). Then again, you could do pizza at **Pequod's** (p74) and blues at **Kingston Mines** (p77) or **BLUES** (p76).

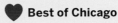

👁 Top Sights

Lincoln Park (p68)

💜 Best of Chicago

Comedy & Performing Arts
Second City (p76)

iO Theater (p76)

Steppenwolf Theatre (p76)

Eating
Alinea (p73)

Pequod's Pizza (p74)

Wiener's Circle (p74)

Drinking & Nightlife
Old Town Ale House (p75)

Delilah's (p75)

J Parker (p75)

Live Music
BLUES (p76)

Kingston Mines (p77)

Lincoln Hall (p77)

Sports & Activities
North Avenue Beach (p72)

Getting There

Ⓜ **El** Brown, Purple, Red Line to Fullerton for Lincoln Park (the neighborhood); Brown, Purple Line to Sedgwick for Old Town.

🚌 **Bus** 151 from downtown for zoo and park sites.

Top Sights
Lincoln Park

The neighborhood gets its name from this park, Chicago's largest. Its 1200 acres stretch for 6 miles, from North Ave north to Diversey Pkwy, where it narrows along the lake and continues until the end of Lake Shore Dr. On sunny days locals come out to play in droves, taking advantage of the ponds, paths and playing fields or visiting the zoo and beaches. It's a fine spot to while away a morning or afternoon (or both).

👁 Map p70, G4

🕐 6am-11pm

🚌 151

Chicago skyline viewed from Lincoln Park

Don't Miss

Zoo & Other Freebies

Opened in 1868, the free Lincoln Park Zoo has entertained generations of Chicagoans. Families swarm the grounds, which are smack in the park's midst. Kids beeline for the Regenstein African exhibit, which puts them close to pygmy hippos and dwarf crocodiles. The Ape House pleases with its swingin' gorillas and chimps. Snow monkeys chill in the Macaque Forest. The leafy conservatory and hidden lily garden are also nearby and free.

Lincoln & the Mausoleum

At the park's southern edge, sculptor Augustus Saint-Gaudens' *Standing Lincoln* shows the 16th president deep in contemplation before giving a speech. Saint-Gaudens based the work on casts made of Lincoln's face and hands while Lincoln was alive. The statue stands behind the Chicago History Museum. Nearby, on the corner of LaSalle Dr and Clark St, take a gander at the Couch Mausoleum. It's the sole reminder of the land's pre-1864 use, when it was a municipal cemetery. Many graves contained dead soldiers from Camp Douglas, a horrific prisoner-of-war stockade on the city's South Side during the Civil War. The city eventually relocated the bodies.

Beaches & Beyond

There's more beyond the zoo, gardens and monuments. Head north and there are sailboat harbors, golf courses, bird sanctuaries and rowing clubs gliding on the lagoons. Walk east from anywhere in the park and you'll come to the Lakefront Trail that connects several beaches along the way.

☑ Top Tips

▶ Markets and take-away joints pop up along Clark St and Diversey Pkwy, prime for picnic provisions.

▶ Convenient Divvy stations to grab a bike for a short ride are on the corner of Lake Shore Dr and North Blvd, and at the Theater on the Lake building (near the intersection of Lake Shore Dr and W Fullerton Pkwy).

▶ Visit the park on Wednesday or Saturday morning to experience Green City Market's bounty as a bonus to your jaunt.

✖ Take a Break

Sultan's Market (p74) does the trick for a casual Middle Eastern meal. The J Parker (p75) provides a swankier break at its rooftop cocktail bar.

A

25

B

15

C

D

12

24

W Wrightwood Ave

1

W Wrightwood Ave

N Lincoln Ave

N Surrey Ct

N Racine Ave

N Seminary Ave

21

W Lill Ave

20

N Halsted St

N Burling St

N Orchard St

W Deming Pl

N Clark St

W Altgeld St

W Montana St

8

W Arlington Pl

Fullerton

22

Biograph
Theater

W Fullerton Ave

7

DePaul Art
Museum

DePaul
University

LINCOLN PARK

2

N Wayne Ave

N Lakewood Ave

N Magnolia Ave

N Racine Ave

N Clifton Ave

W Belden Ave

W Belden Ave

N Geneva Tce

N Cleveland Ave

10

W Webster Ave

N Seminary Ave

N Kenmore Ave

N Sheffield Ave

N Bissell St

N Fremont St

N Dayton St

N Halsted St

Oz Park

N Lincoln Ave

3

W Dickens Ave

N Larrabee St

W Armitage Ave

Armitage

W Cortland St

W Clybourn Ave

N Maud Ave

N Marcey St

N Bissell St

W Wisconsin St

N Burling St

N Orchard St

N Howe St

N Larrabee St

N Mohawk St

4

North Branch Chicago River

N Kingsbury St

W Willow St

W Willow St

OLD TOWN

N Dayton St

W Willow St

9

17

5

W North Ave

North/Clybourn

19

N Lakeview Ave

N Cannon Dr

Diversey Harbor

N Stockton Dr

North Pond

Lincoln Park

N Lake Shore Dr

Fullerton Beach

For reviews see

◉	Top Sights	p68
◉	Sights	p72
✕	Eating	p73
☕	Drinking	p75
★	Entertainment	p76
🔒	Shopping	p77

Peggy Notebaert Nature Museum **5**

W Fullerton Pkwy

Lincoln Park Conservatory **4**

N Clark St

N Lincoln Park W

W Webster Ave

Lincoln Park Zoo **1**

P

W Dickens Ave

Lincoln Park Zoo

N Stockton Dr

South Lagoon

P

N Cannon Dr

Lake Michigan

N Lincoln Ave

W Wisconsin St

South Pond

Lincoln Park

Green City Market

N Hudson Ave

W Menomonee St **16** **6**

N Wells St

N Clark St

Lincoln Park ◉

North Avenue Beach

W Willow St

N Lake Shore Dr

N Hudson Ave

N Sedgwick St

W Eugenie St

13 ✕

W La Salle Dr

Couch Mausoleum

Chicago History Museum **3**

Standing Lincoln Sculpture

2 North Avenue Beach

18 ★

M Sedgwick

W North Ave

14 **11** ✕

23 🔒

N LaSalle Dr

E North Blvd

Archbishop's Residence

Cyrus McCormick Mansion

N Astor St

Sights

Lincoln Park Zoo　　ZOO

1 ⊙ Map p70, F3

The zoo is a local freebie favorite, filled with lions, tigers, snow monkeys and other exotic creatures in the shadow of downtown. Check out the Regenstein African Journey and dragonfly-dappled Nature Boardwalk for the cream of the crop. The Gateway Pavilion (on Cannon Dr) is the main entrance; pick up a map and schedule of feedings and training sessions. (☑312-742-2000; www.lpzoo.org; 2200 N Cannon Dr; admission free; ⊙10am-4:30pm Nov-Mar, to 5pm Apr-Oct, to 6:30pm Sat & Sun Jun-Aug; 🚼; 🚌151)

North Avenue Beach　　BEACH

2 ⊙ Map p70, H4

Chicago's most popular strand of sand wafts a southern California vibe. Buff teams spike volleyballs, kids build sandcastles and everyone jumps in for a swim when the sun hots up. Bands and DJs rock the steamboat-shaped beach house, which serves ice cream and margaritas in equal measure. Kayaks, jet skis, stand-up paddleboards and lounge chairs are available to rent. (www.cpdbeaches.com; 1600 N Lake Shore Dr; 🛜🚼; 🚌151)

Chicago History Museum　　MUSEUM

3 ⊙ Map p70, F5

Curious about Chicago's storied past? Multimedia displays at this museum cover it all, from the Great Fire to the 1968 Democratic Convention. President Lincoln's deathbed is here; the bell from Mrs O'Leary's cow is here. So is the chance to 'become' a Chicago hot dog covered in condiments (in the kids' area, but adults are welcome for the photo op). (☑312-642-4600; www.chicagohistory.org; 1601 N Clark St; adult/child $14/free; ⊙9:30am-4:30pm Mon-Sat, noon-5pm Sun; 🚼; 🚌22)

Lincoln Park Conservatory　　GARDENS

4 ⊙ Map p70, F2

Walking through the conservatory's 3 acres of desert palms, jungle ferns and tropical orchids is like taking a trip around the world in 30 minutes. The glass-bedecked hothouse remains a sultry, 75°F escape, even in winter. (☑312-742-7736; www.lincolnparkconservancy.org; 2391 N Stockton Dr; admission free; ⊙9am-5pm; 🚌151)

Peggy Notebaert Nature Museum　　MUSEUM

5 ⊙ Map p70, F2

This hands-on museum has turtles and croaking frogs in its 1st-floor marsh, fluttering insects in its 2nd-floor butterfly haven and a bird boardwalk meandering through its rooftop garden. It's geared mostly to kids. Check the schedule for daily creature feedings. (☑773-755-5100; www.naturemuseum.org; 2430 N Cannon Dr; adult/child $9/6; ⊙9am-5pm Mon-Fri, 10am-5pm Sat & Sun; 🚼; 🚌151)

Green City Market   MARKET

6 ◉ Map p70, F4

Stands of purple cabbages, red radishes, green asparagus and other bright-hued produce sprawl through Lincoln Park at Chicago's biggest farmers market. Follow your nose to the demonstration tent, where local cooks such as *Top Chef* winner Stephanie Izard prepare dishes – say rice crepes with a mushroom gastrique – using market ingredients. (www.green citymarket.org; 1790 N Clark St; ⊙8am-1pm Wed & Sat May-Oct; ⬜22)

DePaul Art Museum   MUSEUM

7 ◉ Map p70, B2

DePaul University's compact art museum hosts changing exhibits of 20th-century works. Pieces from the permanent collection – by sculptor Claes Oldenburg, cartoonist Chris Ware, architect Daniel Burnham and more – hang on the 2nd floor. It's definitely worth swinging through if you're in the neighborhood; you can see everything in less than 30 minutes. (www.depaul.edu/museum; 935 W Fullerton Ave; admission free; ⊙11am-7pm Wed & Thu, 11am-5pm Fri, noon-5pm Sat & Sun; Ⓜ Brown, Purple, Red Line to Fullerton)

Biograph Theater   HISTORIC SITE

8 ◉ Map p70, C2

In 1934, the 'lady in red' betrayed gangster John Dillinger at the Biograph, which used to show movies. FBI agents shot him in the alley

THE WASHINGTON POST/GETTY IMAGES ©

Cheesecake by Alinea

beside the building. The venue now holds the Victory Gardens Theater, specializing in Chicago-focused plays. (2433 N Lincoln Ave; Ⓜ Brown, Purple, Red Line to Fullerton)

Eating

Alinea   MODERN AMERICAN $$$

9 ✖ Map p70, C5

One of the globe's best restaurants, Alinea brings on 20 courses of mind-bending molecular gastronomy. Dishes may emanate from a centrifuge or be pressed into a capsule, a la duck served with a 'pillow of lavender air.'

There are no reservations. Instead Alinea sells tickets two to three months in advance via its website. Check the Twitter feed (@Alinea) for last-minute seats. (📞312-867-0110; www.alinearestaurant.com; 1723 N Halsted St; multicourse menu $210-265; ⏰5-9:30pm Wed-Sun; Ⓜ Red Line to North/Clybourn)

Pequod's Pizza
PIZZA $

10 🍴 Map p70, A3

Like the ship in *Moby Dick,* from which this neighborhood restaurant takes its name, Pequod's pan-style (akin to deep dish) pizza is a thing of legend – head and shoulders above deep dish competitors because of its caramelized cheese, generous toppings and sweetly flavored sauce. The atmosphere is affably rugged too, with surly waitstaff and graffiti-covered walls. (📞731-327-1512; www.pequodspizza.com; 2207 N Clybourn Ave; small pizzas from $12; ⏰11am-2am Mon-Sat, to midnight Sun; 🚌9 to Webster)

Ⓠ Local Life
Sultan's Market

Neighborhood folks dig the falafel sandwiches, spinach pies and other quality Middle Eastern fare at family-run **Sultan's Market** (Map p70 D1; 📞312-638-9151; www.chicago-falafel.com; 2521 N Clark St; mains $4-7; ⏰10am-10pm Mon-Thu, to midnight Fri & Sat, to 9pm Sun; Ⓜ Brown, Purple, Red Line to Fullerton). The small, homey space doesn't have many tables, but Lincoln Park is nearby for picnicking.

La Fournette
FRENCH $

11 🍴 Map p70, F5

The chef hails from Alsace in France and he fills his narrow, rustic-wood bakery with bright-hued macarons (purple passionfruit, green pistachio, red raspberry-chocolate), cheese-infused breads and crust-crackling baguettes. They all beg to be devoured on the spot with a cup of locally roasted Intelligentsia coffee. Staff make delicious soups, crepes, quiches and sandwiches with equal French love. (📞312-624-9430; www.lafournette.com; 1547 N Wells St; items $3-7; ⏰7am-6:30pm Mon-Sat, to 5:30pm Sun; Ⓜ Brown, Purple Line to Sedgwick)

Wiener's Circle
AMERICAN $

12 🍴 Map p70, D1

As famous for its unruly, foul-mouthed ambiance as its charred hot dogs and cheddar fries, the Wiener's Circle is a scene for late-night munchies. During the day and on weeknights it's a normal hot-dog stand – with damn good food. The wild show is on weekend eves, around 2am, when the nearby bars close and everyone starts yelling. (📞773-477-7444; 2622 N Clark St; hot dogs $3-7; ⏰11am-4am Sun-Thu, to 5am Fri & Sat; Ⓜ Brown, Purple Line to Diversey)

Twin Anchors
BARBECUE $$

13 🍴 Map p70, E5

Twin Anchors is synonymous with ribs – smoky, tangy-sauced baby backs in this case. The meat drops from the ribs as soon as you lift them.

The restaurant doesn't take reservations, so you'll have to wait outside or around the neon-lit 1950s bar, which sets the tone for the place. An almost-all-Sinatra jukebox completes the supper-club ambience. (312-266-1616; www.twinanchorsribs.com; 1655 N Sedgwick St; mains $17-27; ⏰5-11pm Mon-Thu, 5pm-midnight Fri, noon-midnight Sat, noon-10.30pm Sun; Ⓜ Brown, Purple Line to Sedgwick)

Drinking

Old Town Ale House BAR

 14 Map p70, F5

Located across the street from Second City and the scene of late-night musings since the 1960s, this unpretentious neighborhood favorite lets you mingle with beautiful people and grizzled regulars, seated pint by pint under the nude-politician paintings. Classic jazz on the jukebox provides the soundtrack for the jovial goings-on. Cash only (www.theoldtownalehouse.com; 219 W North Ave; ⏰3pm-4am Mon-Fri, from noon Sat & Sun; Ⓜ Brown, Purple Line to Sedgwick)

Delilah's BAR

 15 Map p70, B1

A bartender rightfully referred to this bad-ass black sheep of the neighborhood as the 'pride of Lincoln Ave' – a title earned for the heavy pours and

the best whiskey selection in the city. They know their way around a beer list, too, tapping unusual domestic and international suds (though cheap Pabst longnecks are always behind the bar as well). (🕿773-472-2771; www.delilahschicago.com; 2771 N Lincoln Ave; ⏰4pm-2am Sun-Fri, to 3am Sat; Ⓜ Brown Line to Diversey)

J Parker LOUNGE

 16 Map p70, F4

It's all about the view from the Hotel Lincoln's 13th-floor rooftop bar. And it delivers, sweeping over the park, the lake and downtown skyline. Prepare to jostle with the young and preppy crowd, especially if it's a warm night. (www.jparkerchicago.com; 1816 N Clark St; ⏰5pm-1am Mon-Thu, from 1pm Fri, from 11:30am Sat & Sun; 🚌22)

 Top Tip

Sightseeing from the El

The El train provides a great cheap sightseeing tour of the city. For the best views, hop on the Brown Line and ride into the Loop. Get on in Lincoln Park at either the Fullerton or Armitage stops, take a seat by the window and watch as the train clatters downtown, swinging past skyscrapers so close you can almost touch them.

Old Town Ale House (p75)

Entertainment

Steppenwolf Theatre   THEATER

17 ⭐ Map p70, C5

Steppenwolf is Chicago's top stage for quality, provocative theater productions. The Hollywood-heavy ensemble includes Gary Sinise, John Malkovich, Martha Plimpton, Gary Cole, Joan Allen and Tracy Letts. A money-saving tip: the box office releases 20 tickets for $20 for each day's shows. They go on sale at 11am Tuesday to Saturday and at 1pm Sunday, and are available by phone. (📞312-335-1650; www.steppenwolf.org; 1650 N Halsted St; Ⓜ Red Line to North/Clybourn)

Second City   COMEDY

18 ⭐ Map p70, F5

Bill Murray, Stephen Colbert, Tina Fey and many more honed their wit at this slick venue. The Mainstage and ETC stage host sketch revues (with an improv scene thrown in); they're similar in price and quality. The UP stage hosts stand-up and experimental shows. Bargain: turn up around 10pm (Friday and Saturday excluded) and watch the comics improv a set for free. (📞312-337-3992; www.secondcity.com; 1616 N Wells St; Ⓜ Brown, Purple Line to Sedgwick)

iO Theater   COMEDY

19 ⭐ Map p70, B5

Chicago's other major improv house is a bit edgier than its competition, with four stages hosting bawdy shows nightly. Two bars and a beer garden add to the fun. (📞312-929-2401; ioimprov.com/chicago; 1501 N Kingsbury St; Ⓜ Red Line to North/Clybourn)

BLUES   BLUES

20 ⭐ Map p70, C1

Long, narrow and high volume, this veteran blues club draws a slightly older crowd that soaks up every crackling, electrified moment. As one local musician put it, 'The audience here comes out to *understand* the blues.' Big local names grace the small stage. (www.chicagobluesbar.com; 2519 N Halsted St; cover charge $7-10; ⏰8pm-2am Wed-Sun; Ⓜ Brown, Purple, Red Line to Fullerton)

Kingston Mines   BLUES

21 ⭐ Map p70, C1

Popular enough to draw big names on the blues circuit, Kingston Mines is so noisy, hot and sweaty that blues neophytes will feel as though they're having a genuine experience – sort of like a gritty Delta theme park. Two stages, seven nights a week, ensure somebody's always on. (www.kingston mines.com; 2548 N Halsted St; cover charge $12-15; ☺8pm-4am Mon-Thu, from 7pm Fri & Sat, from 6pm Sun; Ⓜ Brown, Purple, Red Line to Fullerton)

Lincoln Hall   LIVE MUSIC

22 ⭐ Map p70, C2

Hyped national indie bands are the main players at this uber-cool, mid-sized venue with acoustically perfect sound. The front room has a kitchen that offers small plates and sandwiches until 10pm. (☎773-525-2501; www.lincolnhallchicago.com; 2424 N Lincoln Ave; ☒; Ⓜ Brown, Purple, Red Line to Fullerton)

Shopping

Spice House   FOOD

23 🔒 Map p70, F5

A bombardment of fragrance socks you in the nose at this exotic spice house in Old Town, offering delicacies such as black and red volcanic salt from Hawaii and pomegranate molasses among the tidy jars. Best, though, are the house-made herb blends themed after Chicago neighborhoods, such as the Bronzeville Rib Rub, allowing you to take home a taste of the city. (☎312-274-0378; www.thespicehouse.com; 1512 N Wells St; ☺10am-7pm Mon-Sat, to 5pm Sun; Ⓜ Brown, Purple Line to Sedgwick)

Dave's Records   MUSIC

24 🔒 Map p70, D1

Rolling Stone magazine picked Dave's as one of the nation's best record stores. It has an 'all vinyl, all the time' mantra, meaning crate diggers will be in their glory flipping through the stacks of rock, jazz, blues, folk and house. Dave himself usually mans the counter, where you'll find a slew of 25-cent cheapie records for sale. (☎773-929-6325; www.davesrecordschicago.com; 2604 N Clark St; ☺11am-8pm Mon-Sat, noon-7pm Sun; Ⓜ Brown, Purple Line to Diversey)

Rotofugi   TOYS

25 🔒 Map p70, B1

Rotofugi has an unusual niche: urban designer toys. The spacey, robot-y, odd vinyl and plush items will certainly distinguish you from the other kids on the block. It's also a gallery showcasing artists in the fields of modern pop and illustration art. You can usually find locally designed Shawnimals here. (☎773-868-3308; www.rotofugi.com; 2780 N Lincoln Ave; ☺11am-7pm; Ⓜ Brown, Purple Line to Diversey)

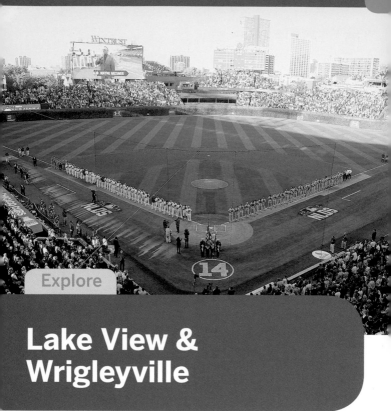

Explore

Lake View & Wrigleyville

Lake View is the overarching name of this good-time neighborhood, inhabited mostly by 20- and 30-somethings. Wrigleyville is the pocket that surrounds star attraction Wrigley Field. It's well mannered by day, with an impish dose of carousing in the countless bars by night. Adding to the fun is Boystown, the well-heeled hub of Chicago's gay community, chockablock with dance clubs.

The Sights in a Day

☀ The neighborhood snoozes in the morning. By 11am places start to open so you can wander Halsted St in **Boystown** (p83), where shops sell naughty knickers and gay novelties, or browse Clark St for fun shops such as **Strange Cargo** (p85). Fuel up with an early lunch at **Crisp** (p83).

☼ In good weather, nothing beats an afternoon at **Wrigley Field** (pictured left; p80). The neighborhood jumps with high-fiving sports fans spilling out of bars. Even if there's not a game on, explore the historic ballpark on a tour.

☾ For dinner, fork into modern comfort food at **Home Bistro** (p83) or pasta plates piled high at **Mia Francesca** (p84), then get ready to party. Mellower types can drink at **Bar Pastoral** (p84) or **Gingerman** (p83). Rock fans should check the schedule at **Metro** (p85), while improv fans should see what's on at **Comedysportz** (p85). Late at night head to **Berlin** (p84) or **Smart Bar** (p84) to shake your tail.

◉ Top Sights
Wrigley Field (p80)

♥ Best of Chicago

Sports & Activities
Chicago Cubs (p85)

Gay & Lesbian
Sidetrack (p84)

Berlin (p84)

Closet (p84)

Home Bistro (p83)

Live Music
Metro (p85)

Drinking & Nightlife
Smart Bar (p84)

Berlin (p84)

Shopping
Strange Cargo (p85)

Comedy & Performing Arts
Comedysportz (p85)

Getting There

Ⓜ **El** Red Line to Addison for Wrigley Field and around; Red, Brown, Purple Line to Belmont for much of Boystown.

Top Sights
Wrigley Field

Built in 1914 and named for the chewing-gum maker, Wrigley Field – aka the Friendly Confines – is the second-oldest baseball park in the major leagues. It's filled with legendary traditions and curses, and has a home team that suffers from the longest dry spell in US sports history. The hapless Cubbies haven't won a championship since 1908, a sad record unmatched in pro football, hockey or basketball.

⊙ Map p82, B3

www.cubs.com

1060 W Addison St

Ⓜ Red Line to Addison

Wrigley Field

Don't Miss

Environs

The ballpark provides an old-school slice of Americana, with a hand-turned scoreboard, ivy-covered outfield walls and an iconic neon sign over the front entrance. The field is uniquely situated smack in the middle of a neighborhood, surrounded on all sides by houses, bars and restaurants. Modern elements have been incorporated recently, including a jumbo-sized video screen in left field.

The Curse

It started with Billy Sianis, owner of the Billy Goat Tavern. The year was 1945 and the Cubs were in the World Series against the Detroit Tigers. When Sianis tried to enter Wrigley Field with his pet goat to see the game, ballpark staff refused, saying the goat stank. Sianis threw up his arms and called down a mighty hex: 'The Cubs will never win another World Series!' And they haven't.

The Traditions

When the middle of the seventh inning arrives, it's time for the seventh inning stretch. You then stand up for the group sing-along of 'Take Me Out to the Ballgame,' typically led by a guest celebrity along the lines of Mr T, Ozzy Osbourne or the local weatherman. Here's another tradition: if you catch a home run slugged by the competition, you're honor-bound to throw it back onto the field. After every game the ballpark hoists a flag atop the scoreboard. A white flag with a blue 'W' indicates a victory; a blue flag with a white 'L' means a loss.

☑ Top Tips

▶ Buy tickets at the Cubs' website or Wrigley box office. Online ticket broker **StubHub** (www.stubhub.com) is also reliable.

▶ The Upper Reserved Infield seats are usually pretty cheap. They're high up, but have decent views.

▶ No tickets? Peep through the 'knothole,' a garage door–sized opening on Sheffield Ave, to watch the action for free on game days.

✗ Take a Break

It's a pre-game ritual to beer up at **Murphy's Bleachers** (Map p82, B3; ☎ 773-281 5356; www.murphysbleachers.com; 3655 N Sheffield Ave; ⏰ 11am-2am; Ⓜ Red Line to Addison), only steps away from the ballpark. Inside Wrigley Field, bite into a gourmet hot dog at the Hot Doug's food stand at Platform 14 (behind the bleachers, though you need a bleacher ticket to get there).

N Kenmore Ave

N Broadway

N Clarendon St

N Lake Shore Dr

Sydney R Marovitz Golf Course

W Bittersweet Pl

0 — 400 m
0 — 0.2 miles

W Irving Park Rd

W Dakin St

Wunders Cemetery

Hebrew Cemetery

W Byron St

Ⓜ Sheridan

W Sheridan Rd

W Byron St

Lincoln Park

N Wayne Ave

N Lakewood Ave

N Clark St

N Seminary Ave

N Kenmore Ave

N Sheffield Ave

N Wilton Ave

N Fremont St

W Grace St

41

N Recreation Dr

4 📷
10 ☆

W Bradley Pl

W Halsted St

N Lake Shore Dr

W Waveland Ave

W Waveland Ave

N Pine Grove Ave

N Recreation Dr

WRIGLEYVILLE

9 ☆

Wrigley Field

N Southport Ave

W Addison St

N Racine Ave

Addison Ⓜ

W Addison St

N Broadway

W Eddy St

W Cornelia Ave

W Cornelia Ave

W Cornelia Ave

W Stratford Pl

Southport
Ⓜ

12 🔒

N Clark St

W Newport Ave

N Elaine Pl

W Hawthorne Pl

W Roscoe St

3 ⊗
W Roscoe St

W Roscoe St

N Southport Ave

W Henderson St

7 ◗

8 ◗

W School St

W Buckingham Pl

BOYSTOWN

W Melrose St

W Aldine Ave

1 ◉

W Belmont Ave

6 ◗

W Belmont Ave

Boystown

W Fletcher St

Belmont Ⓜ

11 ☆

W Briar Pl

LAKE VIEW

N Lakewood Ave

N Racine Ave

N Clifton Ave

N Seminary Ave

N Kenmore Ave

W Barry Ave

W Barry Ave

W Barry Ave

N Broadway

N Clark St

W Wellington Ave

W Wellington Ave

Ⓜ Wellington

2 ⊗ 5 ◗

Sights

Boystown   AREA

1 Map p82, D4

What the Castro is to San Francisco,
Boystown is to the Windy City. The
mecca of queer Chicago (especially
for men), the streets of Boystown are
full of rainbow flags and packed with
bars, shops and restaurants catering
to residents of the gay neighborhood.
(btwn Halsted & Broadway Sts, Belmont Ave &
Addison St; M Red Line to Addison)

Eating

Crisp   ASIAN $

2 Map p82, D5

Music pours from the stereo, and
cheap, delicious Korean fusions arrive
from the kitchen at this cheerful cafe.
The 'Bad Boy Buddha' bowl, a vari-
ation on *bi bim bop* (mixed vegetables
with rice), is one of the best healthy
lunches in town. (www.crisponline.com;
2940 N Broadway; mains $9-13; ☺11:30am-
9pm; M Brown, Purple Line to Wellington)

Home Bistro   MODERN AMERICAN $$

3 Map p82, C4

Home Bistro (aka 'HB') feels as cozy
as the nouveau comfort food it serves.
Beer-soaked mussels, Swiss-style
macaroni and cheese, and buttermilk
fried chicken hit the tables in the
wood-and-tile-lined space. Try to snag
a seat by the front window, which
entertains with Boystown people-

Strange Cargo (p85)

watching. You can bring your own
wine or beer, which is a nice money
saver. (☎773-661-0299; www.homebistro
chicago.com; 3404 N Halsted St; mains $19-
25; ☺5:30-10pm Tue-Thu, 5-10:30pm Fri &
Sat, 11am-9pm Sun; M Red Line to Addison)

Drinking

Gingerman Tavern   BAR

4 Map p82, B2

The pool tables, good beer selection
and pierced-and-tattooed patrons make
Gingerman wonderfully different from
the surrounding Wrigleyville sports
bars. (3740 N Clark St; ☺3pm-2am Mon-Fri,
from noon Sat & Sun; M Red Line to Addison)

Bar Pastoral WINE BAR

5 Map p82, D5

Popular deli minichain Pastoral has a wine bar attached to its Lake View shop. Half-glasses are available for $5, which means you can sample widely. The deli's awesome breads and cheeses help soak it up (stick to these rather than the dishes listed on the menu). (www.barpastoral.com; 2947 N Broadway; ⏰5-10pm Mon-Wed, 5-11pm Thu, 5pm-midnight Fri, 11am-midnight Sat, 11am-10pm Sun; Ⓜ Brown, Purple Line to Wellington)

Smart Bar CLUB

Smart Bar is a long-standing, unpretentious favorite for dancing, in the basement of the Metro rock club (see 10 ✪ Map p82 , B2). The DJs are often more renowned than you'd expect the intimate space to accommodate. (www.smartbarchicago.com; 3730 N Clark St; ⏰10pm-4am Wed-Sun; Ⓜ Red Line to Addison)

Berlin CLUB

6 Map p82, C4

Looking for a packed, sweaty dance floor? Berlin caters to a mostly gay crowd midweek, though partiers of all stripes jam the place on weekends. Monitors flicker through the latest video dispatches from cult pop and electronic acts, while DJs take the dance floor on trancey detours. (📞773-348-4975; www.berlinchicago.com; 954 W Belmont Ave; ⏰10pm-4am Tue, from 5pm Wed-Sun; Ⓜ Red, Brown, Purple Line to Belmont)

Sidetrack CLUB

7 Map p82, C4

Massive Sidetrack thumps dance music for a gay and straight crowd alike. Get ready to belt out your Broadway best at the good-time 'show-tune nights' on Sunday and Monday. If the indoor action gets too much, the huge outdoor courtyard beckons. (www.sidetrackchicago.com; 3349 N Halsted St; ⏰3pm-2am Mon-Fri, from 1pm Sat & Sun; Ⓜ Red, Brown, Purple Line to Belmont)

Closet GAY & LESBIAN

8 Map p82, D4

One of the few lesbian-centric bars in Chicago, the Closet changes mood and tempo at 2am, when the crowd becomes more mixed (male and female), the music gets louder and things get a little rowdier. Cash only. (📞773-477-8533;

Ⓠ Local Life
Mia Francesca

Mia Francesca (Map p82, C4; 📞773-281-3310; www.miafrancesca.com; 3311 N Clark St; mains $16-27; ⏰5-10pm Mon-Thu, to 11pm Fri, 11:30am-11pm Sat, 10am-9pm Sun; Ⓜ Red, Brown, Purple Line to Belmont) buzzes with regulars who come for the trattoria's Italian standards. The handwritten menu features seafood linguine, spinach ravioli, veal medallions and more – all prepared with simple flair and served on white tablecloth tables topped with fresh flowers.

www.theclosetchicago.com; 3325 N Broadway; 4pm-4am Mon-Fri, from noon Sat & Sun; ; Red, Brown, Purple Line to Belmont)

Entertainment

Chicago Cubs
BASEBALL

9 Map p82, B3

The beloved, beleaguered Cubs play at Wrigley Field. It has been more than a century since the team won the World Series, but that doesn't stop fans and tourists from coming out to see their games. Ticket prices vary, but in general you'll be hard-pressed to get in for less than $30. The bleacher seats are the most popular place to sit. (www.cubs.com; 1060 W Addison St; Red Line to Addison)

Metro
LIVE MUSIC

10 Map p82, B2

For more than three decades the Metro has been synonymous with loud rock. Sonic Youth and the Ramones in the '80s. Nirvana and Jane's Addiction in the '90s. White Stripes and The Killers in the new millennium. Each night prepare to hear noise by three or four bands who may well be teetering on the verge of stardom. (www.metrochicago.com; 3730 N Clark St; Red Line to Addison)

Comedysportz
COMEDY

11 Map p82, C5

The gimmick? Two teams compete to make you laugh. It's comedy played

Top Tip

Managing the Wrigleyville Crowds

If there's a Cubs game at Wrigley Field, plan on around 30,000 extra people joining you for a visit to the neighborhood. The trains and buses will be stuffed to capacity, traffic will be snarled, and bars and restaurants will be jam-packed. It can be fun...if that's your scene. If not, you might want to visit on a non-game day for a bit more elbow room.

like a sport (hence the name). The show is totally improvised, with the audience dictating the action. A referee moderates and the wittiest team 'wins' at the end. You can bring in alcohol from the lobby bar. (773-549-8080; www.comedysportzchicago.com; 929 W Belmont Ave; Red, Brown, Purple Line to Belmont)

Shopping

Strange Cargo
CLOTHING

12 Map p82, D3

This retro store stocks hipster wear, platform shoes, wigs and a mindblowing array of kitschy T-shirts. Staff will iron on decals of Harry Caray, Mike Ditka, the Hancock Center or other local touchstones, as well as Obama, Smurfs and more – all supreme souvenirs. (www.strangecargo.com; 3448 N Clark St; 11am-6:45pm Mon-Sat, to 5:30pm Sun; Red Line to Addison)

Local Life
Mixing It Up in Andersonville & Uptown

Getting There

M Red Line to Berwyn (six blocks east of Clark St) for Andersonville. Red Line to Lawrence for Green Mill.

🚌 Number 22 travels along Clark St.

Andersonville is an old Swedish enclave, where timeworn European-tinged businesses mix with new foodie restaurants, antique shops and gay and lesbian bars. Nearby Uptown is a whole different scene, with historic jazz houses such as the Green Mill (Al Capone's fave), along with the thriving eateries of 'Little Saigon.' Both areas are prime to stroll and window-shop, eat and drink.

❶ Hamburger Mary's

Campy **Hamburger Mary's** (www.hamburgermarys.com/chicago; 5400 N Clark St; ⏱11:30am-midnight Sun-Wed, to 1:30am Thu & Fri, to 2:30am Sat) is an LGBT spot that all of Andersonville hangs out at. It serves well-regarded burgers and weekend brunch in the downstairs restaurant, but the action's on the rowdy, booze-soaked patio.

❷ Swedish Bakery

Locals have been getting in line at **Swedish Bakery** (www.swedishbakery.com; 5348 N Clark St; pastries $1.50-4; ⏱6:30am-6:30pm Mon-Fri, to 5pm Sat) for custard-plumped eclairs, French silk tortes and chocolate-chip streusels for more than 80 years. Free samples and coffee help ease the wait.

❸ Big Jones

Warm, sunny **Big Jones** (www.bigjoneschicago.com; 5347 N Clark St; mains $17-25; ⏱11am-9pm Mon-Thu, to 10pm Fri, from 9am Sat & Sun) puts 'southern heirloom cooking' on the menu. Residents flock in for chicken and dumplings, crawfish étouffée and shrimp and grits. The decadent, biscuit-laden brunch draws the biggest crowds.

❹ Woolly Mammoth

Woolly Mammoth Antiques & Oddities (www.woollymammothchicago.com; 1513 W Foster Ave ; ⏱1-7pm Mon, from 3pm Tue, from noon Wed-Sun) is part morbid curiosity shop, part art installation. Creepy doll heads, a stuffed wallaby, jar of old dentures, the record book from an insane asylum – they're all here, and then some.

❺ Hopleaf

A cozy, European-style tavern, **Hopleaf** (www.hopleaf.com; 5148 N Clark St; mains $12-27; ⏱noon-11pm Mon-Thu, to midnight Fri & Sat, to 10pm Sun) is a community favorite for its cashew-butter-and-fig-jam sandwich and house specialty of *frites* and ale-soaked mussels. It also pours 200 types of beers, heavy on the Belgian brew.

❻ Hot G Dog

Hot G Dog (www.hotgdog.com; 5009 N Clark St; hot dogs $2.50-4; ⏱10:30am-8pm Mon-Sat, to 4pm Sun) is the place to bite into, say, a chicken apple cranberry hot dog with whiskey cheese and pecans. It's also a fine place to try a good ol' Chicago-style dog. The chefs formerly worked at Hot Doug's famed shop.

❼ Nha Hang Viet Nam

Little **Nha Hang Viet Nam** (1032 W Argyle St; mains $7-13; ⏱7am-10pm Sun-Mon) may not look like much from the outside, but it offers a huge menu of authentic, well-made dishes from the homeland. It's terrific for pho and clay-pot catfish.

❽ Green Mill

The timeless **Green Mill** (www.greenmill-jazz.com; 4802 N Broadway; ⏱noon-4am Mon-Sat, from 11am Sun) earned its notoriety as Al Capone's favorite speakeasy. Sit in one of the curved leather booths and feel his ghost urging you on to another martini. Local and national jazz artists perform nightly.

Explore

Wicker Park, Bucktown & Ukrainian Village

These three neighborhoods are hot property. Hipster record stores, thrift shops and cocktail lounges have shot up, though vintage Eastern European dive bars linger on many street corners. Wicker Park is the center, buttressed by slightly fancier Bucktown and slightly scruffier Ukrainian Village. The restaurant and rock club scene is unparalleled in the city.

The Sights in a Day

☀ Have a Tex-Mex breakfast at retro diner **Dove's Luncheonette** (p92), then get ready for a hipster shopping spree along Milwaukee and North Aves. Hot spots include **Quimby's** (p96), **Una Mae's** (p97) and **Reckless Records** (p97).

☀ For a change of pace, rise above the commerce by taking a walk on the **606 Trail** (p92). The city converted an old, elevated train track into a groovy walking path. It gives a great feel for the different neighborhoods it traverses.

☽ So many choices for dinner: **Mana Food Bar** (p93) and **Mindy's Hot Chocolate** (pictured left; p93) are in the thick of it. **Ruxbin** (p92) and **Irazu** (p93) are a bit off the beaten path. For drinks, go highbrow with cocktails at the **Violet Hour** (p94). Or opt for a mellower, beer-fueled evening at **Map Room** (p95). You're spoiled for choice when it comes to indie-cool live-music venues. **Hideout** (p95), **Double Door** (p95) and **Empty Bottle** (p96) always have great shows.

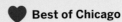 **Best of Chicago**

Eating
Dove's Luncheonette (p92)

Ruxbin (p92)

Mana Food Bar (p93)

Irazu (p93)

Handlebar (p94)

Flo (p94)

Live Music
Hideout (p95)

Empty Bottle (p96)

Double Door (p95)

Drinking & Nightlife
Violet Hour (p94)

Map Room (p95)

Matchbox (p95)

Shopping
Quimby's (p96)

Dusty Groove (p97)

Una Mae's (p97)

Reckless Records (p97)

Getting There

Ⓜ **El** Blue Line to Damen for Bucktown and northern Wicker Park; Blue Line to Division for southern Wicker Park; Blue Line to Chicago for Ukrainian Village.

For reviews see

Sights	p92
Eating	p92
Drinking	p94
Entertainment	p95
Shopping	p96

1 km
0.5 miles

W Fullerton Ave
Fullerton
W Fullerton Ave

N Bissell St
Armitage
N Sheffield Ave
W Armitage Ave
N Maud Ave
N Marcey St
N Kingsbury St
W North Ave
N Magnolia Ave

N Clybourn Ave
W Cortland St
North Branch Chicago River
N Ada St
W Elston Ave
N Elston Ave
15
N Cleaver St

N Ashland Ave
N Ashland Ave
Greenview Ave
N Bosworth Ave

Clybourn
(Metra)
N Marshfield Ave
W Blackhawk St
22

N Elston Ave
John F Kennedy Expwy
N Paulina St
N Hermitage Ave
N Wood St
W Bloomingdale Ave
N Honore Ave
N Wolcott Ave
Churchill Field Park
W Wabansia Ave
W Pierce Ave
W Le Moyne St
W Julian St
W Beach Ave

BUCKTOWN
N Winchester Ave
N Damen Ave
Churchill St
20
WICKER PARK
13
7
3 16
9
W Schiller St

N Webster Ave
N Shakespeare Ave
N Charleston St
N Dickens Ave
N McLean Ave
N Homer St
W Cortland St
N Moffat St
W North Ave
11
Wicker Park
W Evergreen Ave

Holstein Park
12
W Palmer St
N Leavitt St
W Armitage Ave
W Pierce Ave
N Hoyne Ave

W Lyndale St
N Belden Ave
N Medill Ave
94
90

Western
6
N Wilmot Ave
N Milwaukee Ave
N Leavitt St
N Bell Ave
W Wabansia Ave
N Claremont Ave
N Oakley Ave
10
W Le Moyne St
W Hirsch St

Sights

Intuit: The Center for Intuitive & Outsider Art
GALLERY

1 Map p90, E7

Behold the museum-like collection of folk art, including watercolors by famed local Henry Darger. In fact, Intuit has re-created his studio, complete with comic books and welded-can sculptures. (www.art.org; 756 N Milwaukee Ave; admission $5; ☉11am-6pm Tue-Sat, to 7:30pm Thu, noon-5pm Sun; Ⓜ Blue Line to Chicago)

Ukrainian Institute of Modern Art
MUSEUM

2 ◎ Map p90, A6

Step into the bright white storefront and make a choice. To the right is the permanent collection of mod, colorful paintings and sculptures (which rotates a few times per year). To the left are the playful and provocative temporary exhibits, done in various media. While most artists are Ukrainian, plenty of locals get shelf space, too. (☎773-227-5522; www.uima-chicago.org; 2320 W Chicago Ave; admission free; ☉noon-4pm Wed-Sun; 🚌66)

Eating

Dove's Luncheonette
TEX-MEX $

3 🍴 Map p90, B4

Grab a seat at the counter for plates of pork shoulder pozole and shrimp-stuffed sweet corn tamales. Dessert? It's pie, of course, maybe lemon cream or peach jalapeno, depending on what they've baked that day. Soul music spins on a record player, tequila flows from the 70 bottles behind the bar, and presto: all is right in the world. (☎773-645-4060; www.doveschicago.com; 1545 N Damen Ave; mains $12-15; ☉9am-10pm Sun-Thu, to 11pm Fri & Sat; Ⓜ Blue Line to Damen)

Ruxbin
MODERN AMERICAN $$$

4 🍴 Map p90, C6

The passion of the Kim family, who run Ruxbin, is evident in everything from the decor made of found items, such as antique theater seats and church pews, to the artfully prepared flavors on the small, ever-changing, hyper-local menu. It's a wee place of just 32 seats, and BYO. (☎312-624-8509; www.ruxbinchicago.com; 851 N Ashland Ave; mains $27-32; ☉6-10pm Tue-Fri, 5:30-10pm Sat, to 9pm Sun; Ⓜ Blue Line to Division)

Ⓠ Local Life
The 606 Trail

Like NYC's High Line, Chicago's **606** (Map p90, B3; www.the606.org; ☉6am-11pm; Ⓜ Blue Line to Damen) is a similar urban-cool elevated path along an old train track. Bike or stroll past factories, smokestacks, clattering El trains and locals' backyard affairs for 2.7 miles between Wicker Park and Logan Sq. The entrance at Churchill Park (1825 N Damen Ave) is handy to ascend.

Mana Food Bar VEGETARIAN $$

5 Map p90, C5

What's unique here is the focus on creating global dishes without using fake meats. So you won't find soy chorizo or tempeh reubens, but rather multiethnic veggie dishes from the likes of Japan, Korea, Italy and the American Southwest. Beer, smoothies and sake cocktails help wash it down. The small, sleek eatery buzzes, so reserve ahead or prepare to wait. (☎773-342-1742; www.manafoodbar.com; 1742 W Division St; small plates $7-16; ⏱4-10pm Sun-Thu, 4-11pm Fri, noon-11pm Sat; Ⓜ Blue Line to Division)

Irazu LATIN AMERICAN $

6 Map p90, A2

Chicago's unassuming lone Costa Rican eatery turns out burritos bursting with chicken, black beans and fresh avocado, and sandwiches dressed in a heavenly, spicy-sweet vegetable sauce. Wash them down with an *avena* (a slurpable oatmeal milkshake). For breakfast, the *arroz con huevos* (peppery eggs scrambled into rice) relieves hangovers. Irazu is BYO with no corkage fee. Cash only. (☎773-252-5687, www.irazuchicago.com; 1865 N Milwaukee Ave; mains $11-15; ⏱11:30am-9:30pm Mon-Sat; Ⓜ Blue Line to Western)

Mindy's Hot Chocolate AMERICAN $$

7 Map p90, B3

'Come for dessert, stay for dinner' might be the motto at this mod

Hideout (p95)

restaurant helmed by renowned pastry chef Mindy Segal. With nine kinds of hot chocolate available (they're like dipping your mug into Willy Wonka's chocolate river), along with cakes, cookies and mini-brioche doughnuts, you may forget to order the caramel-roasted chicken, crab spaghetti and other entrees on offer. (☎773-489-1747; www.hotchocolatechicago.com; 1747 N Damen Ave; mains $18-30; ⏱11:30am-2pm & 5:30-10pm Tue-Fri, from 10am Sat & Sun; Ⓜ Blue Line to Damen)

Enoteca Roma

ITALIAN $$

8 Map p90, A5

Candlelit and cozy, family-run Enoteca Roma feels like an old country ristorante. Bruschetta flights and handmade pastas steal the show, best consumed on the starry back patio in summer. During the day, sibling eatery Letizia's Natural Bakery wafts toasty panini, lemon tarts and lattes next door. (☑773-772-7700; www.enotecaroma. com; 2146 W Division St; mains $11-18; ☺5-10pm Mon-Thu, to 11pm Fri & Sat, 2:30-9pm Sun; Ⓜ Blue Line to Damen)

Big Star Taqueria

MEXICAN $

9 Map p90, B4

Once a filling station, now a taco-serving honky-tonk bar helmed by a big-name Chicago chef (Paul Kahan). So goes gentrification in Wicker Park. The place gets packed, but damn, those tacos are worth the wait – pork belly in tomato-guajillo chili sauce and mole-spiced carrots drizzled with date-infused yogurt accompany the specialty whiskey list. Cash only. (☑773-235-4039; www.bigstarchicago.com; 1531 N Damen Ave; tacos $3-4; ☺11:30am-1:30am Sun-Thu, to 2:30am Fri & Sat; Ⓜ Blue Line to Damen)

Handlebar

INTERNATIONAL $

10 Map p90, A4

The cult of the bike messenger runs strong in Chicago, and this clamorous restaurant-bar is a way station for tattooed couriers and locals who come for the microbrew-centric beer list, vegetarian-friendly food (including West African groundnut stew and fried avocado tacos) and festive back beer garden. (☑773-384-9546; www. handlebarchicago.com; 2311 W North Ave; mains $9-15; ☺10am-midnight Mon-Fri, from 9am Sat & Sun; ☑; Ⓜ Blue Line to Damen)

Drinking

Violet Hour

COCKTAIL BAR

11 Map p90, B4

This nouveau speakeasy isn't marked, so look for the mural-slathered, wood-panel building and the door topped by a yellow lightbulb. Inside, high-backed booths, chandeliers and long velvet drapes provide the backdrop to elaborately engineered cocktails that the Beard Awards deemed best in the US. The Armageddon (lemon-and-cinnamon-tinged whiskey) shows why. As highbrow as it sounds, Violet Hour

Local Life

Flo

Think you've had a good breakfast burrito before? Not until you've eaten at **Flo** (Map p90, D6; ☑312-243-0477; www.flochicago.com; 1434 W Chicago Ave; mains $12-16; ☺8:30am-10pm Tue-Thu, 8:30am-11pm Fri, 9am-11pm Sat, 9am-3pm Sun; Ⓜ Blue Line to Chicago). The Southwestern-bent dishes and jovial staff draw hordes of late-rising neighborhood hipsters on weekends. Potent margaritas and fish tacos take over after dark.

is welcoming and accessible. (📞773-252-1500; www.thevioletthour.com; 1520 N Damen Ave; ⏰6pm-2am Sun-Fri, to 3am Sat; Ⓜ Blue Line to Damen)

Map Room
BAR

12 Map p90, B2

At this map- and globe-filled 'travelers' tavern,' artsy types sip coffee by day and suds from the 200-strong beer list by night. Board games and old issues of *National Geographic* are within reach for entertainment. (www.maproom.com; 1949 N Hoyne Ave; ⏰6:30am-2am Mon-Fri, from 7:30am Sat, from 11am Sun; 🛜; Ⓜ Blue Line to Western)

Danny's
BAR

13 Map p90, B2

Danny's comfortably dim and dog-eared ambiance is perfect for conversations over a pint early on, then DJs arrive to stoke the dance party as the evening progresses. Cash only. (1951 W Dickens Ave; ⏰7pm-2am; Ⓜ Blue Line to Damen)

Matchbox
BAR

14 Map p90, E6

Lawyers, artists and bums all squeeze in for retro cocktails. It's as small as – you got it – a matchbox, with about 10 barstools; everyone else stands against the back wall. Barkeeps make the drinks from scratch. Favorites include the pisco sour and the ginger gimlet, ladled from an amber vat of homemade ginger-infused vodka. (770 N Milwaukee Ave; ⏰4pm-2am Mon-Fri, from 3pm Sat & Sun; Ⓜ Blue Line to Chicago)

 Local Life
Happy Village

Happy Village (Map p90, B5; www.happyvillagebar.com; 1059 N Wolcott Ave; ⏰4pm-2am Mon-Fri, from noon Sat & Sun; Ⓜ Blue Line to Division) may well be the jolliest bar in the neighborhood. Unapologetically divey, with cheap, non–craft beer, it earns smiles from the fierce table tennis matches, starry vine-covered patio and strolling tamale vendor who seems to appear just when you need him most.

Entertainment

Hideout
LIVE MUSIC

15 ⭐ Map p90, D3

Hidden behind a factory at the edge of Bucktown, this two-room lodge of indie rock and alt-country is well worth seeking out. The owners have nursed an outsider, underground vibe, and the place feels like the downstairs of your grandma's rumpus room. Music and other events (bingo, literary readings etc) take place nightly. (www.hideoutchicago.com; 1354 W Wabansia Ave; ⏰7pm-2am Tue, 4pm-2am Wed-Fri, 7pm-3am Sat, varies Sun & Mon; 🚌72)

Double Door
LIVE MUSIC

16 ⭐ Map p90, B4

Alternative rock that's *just* under the radar finds a home at this former liquor store, which still has the original sign out front and remains

Quimby's

a landmark around the Wicker Park bustle. The cachet is such that groups like the Rolling Stones have plugged in, too. (www.doubledoor.com; 1572 N Milwaukee Ave; Ⓜ Blue Line to Damen)

Empty Bottle
LIVE MUSIC

17 ⭐ Map p90, A5

Chicago's music insiders fawn over the Empty Bottle, the city's scruffy, go-to club for edgy indie rock, jazz and other beats. Monday's show often is a freebie by a couple of up-and-coming bands. Cheap beer, a photo booth and good graffiti reading in the bathrooms add to the dive-bar fun. (www.emptybottle.

com; 1035 N Western Ave; ⏱ 5pm–2am Mon-Thu, from 3pm Fri, from 11am Sat & Sun; 🚌 49)

Chopin Theatre
THEATER

18 ⭐ Map p90, C5

Looking for a tasty slice of Chicago fringe theater? Maybe something odd-ball, thought provoking or just plain silly? Chopin is the place. The city's best itinerant companies, such as House Theatre and Theater Oobleck, often turn up here. (☎ 773-278-1500; www.chopintheatre.com; 1543 W Division St; Ⓜ Blue Line to Division)

Phyllis' Musical Inn
LIVE MUSIC

19 ⭐ Map p90, C5

One of the all-time great dives, this former Polish polka bar features scrappy up-and-coming bands nightly. It's hit or miss for quality, but you've got to applaud them for taking a chance. If you don't like the sound you can always slip outside to the bar's basketball court for relief. Cheap brewskis, to boot. (☎ 773-486-9862; 1800 W Division St; ⏱ 4pm–2am Mon-Fri, from 3pm Sat, from 2pm Sun; Ⓜ Blue Line to Division)

Shopping

Quimby's
BOOKS

20 🔒 Map p90, B3

The epicenter of Chicago's comic and zine worlds, Quimby's is one of the linchpins of underground culture in the city. Here you can find everything from crayon-powered punk-rock manifestos to slickly produced graphic novels. It's a groovy place for cheeky literary souvenirs and bizarro readings. (www.quimbys.com; 1854 W North Ave; ⊙noon-9pm Mon-Thu, to 10pm Fri & Sat, to 7pm Sun; Ⓜ Blue Line to Damen)

Dusty Groove

MUSIC

21 🔒 Map p90, C5

Old-school soul, Brazilian beats, Hungarian disco, bass-stabbing hip-hop – if it's funky, Dusty Groove (which also has its own record label) stocks it. Flip through stacks of vinyl, or get lost amid the tidy shop's CDs. Be sure to check out the dollar bin. (☎773-342-5800; www.dustygroove.com; 1120 N Ashland Ave; ⊙10am-8pm; Ⓜ Blue Line to Division)

Reckless Records

MUSIC

22 🔒 Map p90, C4

Chicago's best indie-rock record and CD emporium allows you to listen to everything before you buy. It's certainly the place to get your finger on the pulse of the local, *au courant* underground scene. There's plenty of elbow room in the big, sunny space, which makes for happy hunting. (☎773-235-3727; www.reckless.com; 1379 N Milwaukee Ave; ⊙10am-10pm Mon-Sat, to 8pm Sun; Ⓜ Blue Line to Damen)

Ⓠ Local Life
Una Mae's

The quarter-mile stretch of Milwaukee Ave between North and Wolcott Aves holds around 10 vintage and thrift shops, punctuated by several funky shoe stores. **Una Mae's** (Map p90, B4; ☎773-276-7002; www.unamaeschicago.com; 1528 N Milwaukee Ave; ⊙noon-8pm Mon-Fri, 11am-8pm Sat, noon-7pm Sun; Ⓜ Blue Line to Damen) is a favorite for its vintage wares and collection of new, cool-cat designer duds.

Wicker Park Secret Agent Supply Co

GIFTS

23 🔒 Map p90, C5

This place sells 'espionagical wares' (aka crazy spy gear). Mustache disguise kits, underwater voice amplifiers, banana-shaped cases to hide your cell phone in – it's genius. Better yet: profits from sales go toward supporting the after-school writing and tutoring programs that take place on-site at nonprofit group 826CHI. (☎773-772-8108; www.826chi.org; 1276 N Milwaukee Ave; ⊙noon-5pm Sun & Mon, 11am-6pm Tue-Sat; 🚻; Ⓜ Blue Line to Division)

Local Life
A Night Out in Logan Square

Getting There

M Blue Line to Logan Square (for places north of Fullerton Ave) or California (for places south of Fullerton).

Logan Square has become the 'it' 'hood for new and cool. But it's also refreshingly low-key, as it remains off the beaten path. Street art displays, unassuming Michelin-starred taverns and dive bars chock-full of local color dot the leafy boulevards. Try to arrive early in the evening to take advantage of the shops and galleries.

❶ Revolution Brewing

Raise your fist to **Revolution** (www.revbrew.com; 2323 N Milwaukee Ave; ⏰11am-2am Mon-Fri, from 10am Sat & Sun), a big, buzzy, industrial-chic brewpub that serves as the neighborhood clubhouse. The brewmaster led the way for Chicago's craft-beer scene, and his suds are top notch. The haute pub grub includes fig-and-pancetta pizza and bacon-fat popcorn with fried sage.

❷ Cole's

Cole's (www.coleschicago.com; 2338 N Milwaukee Ave; ⏰5:30pm-2am Mon-Fri, from 4pm Sat & Sun) is a dive bar with nifty free entertainment. Scenesters flock in to shoot pool and swill Midwest microbrews in the neon-bathed front room. Then they head to the backroom stage where bands and DJs do their thing. On Wednesdays the comedy open mic takes over.

❸ Galerie F

Galerie F (www.galerief.com; 2381 N Milwaukee Ave; ⏰11am-6pm Tue-Sun) is exactly the type of laid-back, uber-cool gallery you'd expect to find in Logan Square. It specializes in rock-and-roll gig posters, printmaking and street art. The vibe is totally welcoming. It sometimes stays open late for exhibition premieres.

❹ Whistler

Hometown indie bands and jazz combos rock wee, arty **Whistler** (www.whistlerchicago.com; 2421 N Milwaukee Ave; admission free; ⏰6pm-2am Mon-Thu, from 5pm Fri-Sun) most nights. There's never a cover charge, but you'd be a shmuck if you didn't order at least one of the swanky cocktails to keep the scene going. Whistler is also a gallery: the front window showcases local artists' work.

❺ Wolfbait & B-girls

Old ironing boards serve as display tables; tape measures, scissors and other designers' tools hang from vintage hooks. You get that crafting feeling as soon as you walk in, and indeed, **Wolfbait & B-girls** (www.wolfbaitchicago.com; 3131 W Logan Blvd; ⏰10am-7pm Mon-Sat, to 6pm Sun) sells the handmade wares (dresses, handbags and jewelry) of local indie designers.

❻ Longman & Eagle

Hard to say whether shabby-chic tavern **Longman & Eagle** (www.longmanandeagle.com; 2657 N Kedzie Ave; mains $15-30; ⏰9am-2am Sun-Fri, to 3am Sat) is best for eating or drinking. Let's say eating, since it earned a Michelin star for its beautifully cooked comfort foods such as wild-boar sloppy joes and fried chicken and duck fat biscuits.

❼ Lost Lake

Hipsters love a good tiki bar, so **Lost Lake** (www.lostlaketiki.com; 3154 W Diversey Ave; ⏰4pm-2am Sun-Fri, to 3am Sat) popped up in 2015 to meet the need. Take a seat under the bamboo roof, by the banana leaf wallpaper, and swirl a Mystery Gardenia or other tropical drink made from one of the 275 rums on offer.

Explore

Near West Side & Pilsen

The Near West Side covers a large swath including Greektown and the booming West Loop. Here chic restaurants, clubs and galleries poke out between meat-processing plants, and it seems like a new, all-the-rage chef opens an eatery (or two) weekly. Nearby in Pilsen, Mexican culture mixes with Chicago's bohemian underground, and colorful murals, taquerias and cafes result.

The Sights in a Day

 A tough breakfast decision awaits: **Lou Mitchell's** (p107) has Milk Duds and convenience going for it. **Sweet Maple Cafe** (p108) has biscuits and grits, but it's a bit far flung. If it's the last weekend of the month, **Randolph Street Market** (p109) is a big to-do.

Take the train to Pilsen. The **National Museum of Mexican Art** (p106) has terrific (and free) exhibits, while 18th St rolls out groovy shops like **Knee Deep Vintage** (p109) and **Comet Vintage** (p109). They share the sidewalk with **Don Pedro Carnitas** (p107), **La Catrina Cafe** (p108) and other Mexican spots, as well as hipster halls such as **Dusek's** (p107).

The West Loop is one of Chicago's richest zones for dinner. But you won't be the only one with the idea. Try for reservations at **Girl and the Goat** (p106) or **Little Goat** (p106), or get in line at **Avec** (p106). Bubbly drinks at **RM Champagne Salon** (p108) is a fine finale.

For a local's day in the West Loop, see p102.

 Local Life

West Loop Wander (p102)

 Best of Chicago

Eating

Girl and the Goat (p106)

Sweet Maple Cafe (p108)

Publican Quality Meats (p103)

Meli Cafe (p107)

Museums & Galleries

National Museum of Mexican Art (p106)

Mars Gallery (p102)

Shopping

Knee Deep Vintage (p109)

For Kids

Lou Mitchell's (p107)

Getting There

Ⓜ **El** Pink Line to 18th St for Pilsen; Green, Pink Line to Morgan or Clinton for West Loop

🚌 **Bus** Numbers 19 (game-day express) and 20 for United Center.

Q Local Life
West Loop Wander

The West Loop has exploded in the last few years with hot-chef restaurants and condos carved from old meatpacking warehouses. Meat is still the main biz around here, and you're guaranteed to see at least one bloody-apron-clad worker as you traverse the galleries, shops and mega-stylish eateries.

❶ Cool Cat Gallery

Pop-art-filled **Mars Gallery** (www.marsgallery.com; 1139 W Fulton Market; ⊙noon-6pm Wed & Fri, noon-7pm Thu, 11am-5pm Sat; Ⓜ Green, Pink Line to Morgan) is pure fun, from the plaid-tie-wearing cat who roams the premises (he's the assistant manager) to the building's offbeat history (it was an egg factory, then a club where the Ramones played). Bonus: it sits atop an energy vortex.

2 Meat Treat

Neighborhood dwellers come to **Publican Quality Meats** (www.publicanqualitymeats.com; 825 W Fulton Market; mains $8-12; 10am-6pm Mon-Fri, 9am-6pm Sat, 9am-5pm Sun; M Green, Pink Line to Morgan) for its supply of smoked chorizo and maple breakfast sausage. Then they pull up a chair in the small restaurant in the back and linger over beer and artisanal sandwiches.

3 Glazed and Infused

Chicagoans love a good doughnut, and **Glazed and Infused** (www.goglazed.com; 813 W Fulton Market; doughnuts $2-3; 7am-2pm Mon-Thu, to 5pm Fri, to 3pm Sat & Sun; M Green, Pink Line to Morgan) makes them right. That first bite of the vanilla crème brûlée yeast ring, when you crunch into the delicate sugar crust, hooks you for life.

4 Historic Suds

Haymarket Pub & Brewery (www.haymarketbrewing.com; 737 W Randolph St; 11am-2am; M Green, Pink Line to Clinton) provides a nice dose of local history. It's located near where the 1886 Haymarket labor riot took place, and the brewery's suds have affiliated names, such as the Mathias Imperial IPA (named after the first police officer to die in the melee).

5 Community Gallery

threewalls (www.three-walls.org; 119 N Peoria St; 11am-5pm Tue-Sat; M Green, Pink Line to Morgan) is such a groovy gallery it has CSA (community supported art), where locals buy a 'share' and receive an allotment of art (maybe a handwoven placement and ceramic dish). The friendly space hosts great exhibitions.

6 Grocery Grazing

West Loopers shop for their groceries at multi-level **Mariano's** (www.marianos.com; 40 S Halsted St; 6am-10pm; M Blue Line to UIC-Halsted). Pick up something cool to drink or a gelato at the cafe to take for a picnic in the park.

7 Park Stroll

The neighborhood's stroller-pushing families and dog-walking hipsters get their exercise in **Mary Bartelme Park** (115 S Sangamon St; M Blue Line to UIC-Halsted). Five off-kilter stainless-steel arches form the gateway; kids play in the mist that the sculptures release in summer. Grassy mounds dot the park and provide lookout points to view the Willis Tower rising in the distance.

8 Greek Delights

Chicago's small but busy Greektown centers on Halsted St. Residents head to **Artopolis Bakery & Cafe** (312-559-9000; www.artopolischicago.com; 306 S Halsted St; mains $9-15; 9am-midnight Mon-Thu, 9am-1am Fri & Sat, 10am-11pm Sun; M Blue Line to UIC-Halsted) for classics like baklava and spinach-and-feta pies. The cafe-bar opens onto the street, with wine-laden tables along the front.

For reviews see

⊙	Sights	p106
✕	Eating	p106
❶	Drinking	p108
★	Entertainment	p109
⊞	Shopping	p109

PILSEN

National Museum of Mexican Art

Dan Ryan Expwy

Halsted St (Metra)

South Branch Chicago River

W Cermak Rd

Addams Park

Harrison Park

500 m
0.25 miles

Sights

National Museum of Mexican Art
MUSEUM

1 ⊙ Map p104, A6

Founded in 1982, this vibrant museum – the largest Latino arts institution in the USA – has become one of the city's best. The vivid permanent collection sums up 1000 years of Mexican art and culture through classical paintings, skeleton-rich folk art, beadwork and much more. (📞312-738-1503; www. nationalmuseumofmexicanart.org; 1852 W 19th St; admission free; ⏰10am-5pm Tue-Sun; Ⓜ Pink Line to 18th St)

Eating

Little Goat
DINER $$

2 ✖ Map p104, D1

Top Chef winner Stephanie Izard opened this diner for the foodie masses across the street from her ever-booked main restaurant, Girl and the Goat. Scooch into a vintage booth and order off the all-day breakfast menu. Better yet, try lunch and dinner favorites such as the goat sloppy joe with rosemary slaw or the pork belly on scallion pancakes. Izard's flavor combinations rule. (📞312-888-3455; www.littlegoatchicago.com; 820 W Randolph St; mains $10-19; ⏰7am-10pm Sun-Thu, to midnight Fri & Sat; 🛜✒; Ⓜ Green, Pink Line to Morgan)

Girl & the Goat
MODERN AMERICAN $$$

3 ✖ Map p104, D1

Stephanie Izard's flagship restaurant rocks. The soaring ceilings, polished wood tables and cartoony art on the walls offer a convivial atmosphere where local beer and house-made wine hit the tables along with unique small plates such as scallops with brown butter kimchi. Reservations are difficult; try for walk-in seats before 5pm or see if anything opens up at the bar. (📞312-492-6262; www.girlandthegoat. com; 809 W Randolph St; small plates $9-16; ⏰4:30-11pm Sun-Thu, to midnight Fri & Sat; ✒; Ⓜ Green, Pink Line to Morgan)

Avec
MEDITERRANEAN $$

4 ✖ Map p104, E1

Feeling social? This happening spot gives diners a chance to rub elbows at eight-person communal tables. The mini room looks a heck of a lot like a Finnish sauna and fills with noisy chatter as stylish urbanites pile in. The bacon-wrapped dates are the menu's must. The squid-ink pasta and salumi plates beg for your fork, as well. No reservations. (📞312-377-2002; www.avecrestaurant.com; 615 W Randolph St; mains $18-26; ⏰11:30am-2pm & 3:30pm-midnight Mon-Fri, 3:30pm-1am Sat, 10am-2pm & 3:30pm-midnight Sun; Ⓜ Green, Pink Line to Clinton)

Dusek's
MODERN AMERICAN **$$$**

5 Map p104, C6

Pilsen's hipsters gather under the pressed tin ceiling of this gastropub to fork into the ever-changing menu of beer-inspired dishes, such as beer-battered soft shell crab or dark-lager-roasted duck. The eatery shares its historic building with an indie band concert hall and basement cocktail bar. (312-526-3851; www.dusekschicago. com; 1227 W 18th St; mains $22-30; 11am-1am Mon-Fri, from 9am Sat & Sun; M Pink Line to 18th St)

Lou Mitchell's
BREAKFAST **$**

6 Map p104, E2

A relic of Route 66, Lou's brings in elbow-to-elbow locals and tourists for breakfast. The old-school waitresses deliver fluffy omelets that hang off the plate and thick-cut French toast with a jug of syrup. They call you 'honey' and fill your coffee cup endlessly. There's often a queue to get in, but free dough-nut holes and Milk Duds help ease the wait. (312-939-3111; www.loumitchellsres-taurant.com; 565 W Jackson Blvd; mains $7-11; 5:30am-3pm Mon Fri, 7am 3pm Sat & Sun; ; M Blue Line to Clinton)

Don Pedro Carnitas
MEXICAN **$**

7 Map p104, D6

At this no-frills meat den, a man with a machete salutes you at the front counter. He awaits your command to hack off pork pieces, then wraps the thick chunks with onion and cilantro

Restaurant facade in Pilsen

in a fresh tortilla. You then devour the taco at the tables in back. Goat stew and tripe add to the meaty menu. Cash only. (1113 W 18th St; tacos $1.50-2; 6am-6pm Mon-Fri, 5am-5pm Sat, to 3pm Sun; M Pink Line to 18th)

Meli Cafe
BREAKFAST **$$**

8 Map p104, E2

Meli is the Greek word for 'honey,' and it's apt for this sweet breakfast spot. Skillet dishes made from cage-free eggs (served over a bed of potatoes), goat cheese and fig omelets, and the deca-dent French toast (made from challah bread dipped in vanilla-bean custard) start the day off right. Meli has a few outposts around town. (📞312-454-0748; www.melicafe.com; 301 S Halsted St; mains $12-18; 🕙6am-3pm; Ⓜ Blue Line to UIC-Halsted)

Drinking

Goose Island Brewery   BREWERY

9 🚇 Map p104, A1

Goose Island – Chicago's first craft brewer, launched in 1988 – is now owned by Anheuser-Busch InBev, so technically it's no longer a craft brewer. But it still acts like one, making excellent small-batch beers at this facility. The swanky mod-industrial tap room pours eight varieties; sour beers feature on Saturdays. Forty-five-minute tours ($12) are available if you reserve in advance. (www.gooseisland. com; 1800 W Fulton St; 🕙2-8pm Thu & Fri, noon-6pm Sun; Ⓜ Green, Pink Line to Ashland)

🅠 Local Life
Sweet Maple Cafe

The creaking floorboards, matronly staff and soulful home cookin' lend **Sweet Maple Cafe** (Map p104, C4; 📞312-243-8908; www.sweetmaplecafe. com; 1339 W Taylor St; mains $9-12; 🕙7am-2pm; Ⓜ Blue Line to Racine) the bucolic appeal of a Southern roadside diner. The signature dishes – inch-thick banana pancakes, cheddar grits and fluffy biscuits that come smothered in spicy sausage gravy – earn the superlatives of locals.

Skylark   BAR

10 🚇 Map p104, E7

The Skylark is a bastion for artsy drunkards, who slouch into big booths sipping on strong drinks and eyeing the long room. They play pinball, snap pics in the photo booth and scarf down the kitchen's awesome tater tots. Cash only. (📞312-948-5275; www.skylarkchicago. com; 2149 S Halsted St; 🕙4pm-2am; 🚌8)

RM Champagne Salon   BAR

11 🚇 Map p104, D1

This West Loop spot is a twinkling light charmer for bubbles. Score a table in the cobblestoned courtyard and you'll feel transported to Paris. (📞312-243-1199; www.rmchampagnesalon.com; 116 N Green St; 🕙5-11pm Mon-Wed, to 2am Thu & Fri, to 3am Sat, to 11pm Sun; Ⓜ Green, Pink Line to Morgan)

La Catrina Cafe   CAFE

12 🚇 Map p104, D6

Activists, artists and students congregate here for the roomy window seats, bottomless cups of coffee and funky art exhibitions. It's a come-one, come-all kind of spot, prime for a Mexican hot chocolate and Frida Kahlo–face cookie. A colorful mural marks the entrance. (www.lacatrinacafe.com; 1011 W 18th St; 🕙7am-9pm Mon-Thu, 8am-6pm Fri-Sun; 📶; Ⓜ Pink Line to 18th St)

Entertainment

Thalia Hall
LIVE MUSIC

13 ⭐ Map p104, C6

It hosts a cool-cat slate of rock, alt-country, jazz and metal in an ornate 1892 hall patterned after Prague's opera house. A great gastropub on the 1st floor and cocktail bar in the basement invite lingering before and after shows. (www.thaliahallchicago.com; 1807 S Allport St; M Pink Line to 18th St)

Chicago Blackhawks
SPECTATOR SPORT

14 ⭐ Map p104, A2

The Hawks skate at United Center. Tickets have become difficult to get, with lots of sellouts since the team's recent Stanley Cup wins (in 2010, 2013 and 2015). Be sure to arrive in time for the national anthem(s) at the game's start. The raucous, ear-splitting rendition is a tradition. Express bus number 19 plies Madison St on game days. (www.blackhawks.nhl.com; 1901 W Madison St; 🚌 19, 20)

Chicago Bulls
BASKETBALL

15 ⭐ Map p104, A2

They may not be the mythical champions of yore, but the Bulls still draw good crowds at their United Center home base. (www.nba.com/bulls; 1901 W Madison St; 🚌 19, 20)

🔍 Local Life
Pilsen's Vintage Jackpot

Fashionistas know the place to go for fringe jackets or Jackie O-style scarves is 18th St in Pilsen. Several vintage shops dot the mile-long stretch between Halsted St and Ashland Ave. Top of the heap are **Knee Deep Vintage** (Map p104, C6; www.kneedeepvintage.com; 1425 W 18th St; 🕐 noon-8pm Mon-Thu, 11am-9pm Fri & Sat, noon-6pm Sun; M Pink Line to 18th St) and **Comet Vintage** (Map p104, C6; www.cometvintagechicago.com; 1320 W 18th St; 🕐 noon-6pm Sun & Mon, noon-7pm Tue-Thu, 11am-8pm Fri & Sat; M Pink Line to 18th St), both specializing in clothing and homewares from the 1920s to the 1970s, with wares for men and women.

Shopping

Randolph Street Market
MARKET

16 🔒 Map p104, C1

This market, which styles itself on London's Portobello Market, has become quite the to-do in town. It takes place inside the beaux-arts Plumbers Hall, where more than 200 antique dealers hock collectibles, jewelry, furniture, books, rugs and pinball machines. The city's fledgling fashion designers sell their one-of-a-kind skirts, shawls and handbags in the Indie Designer Market section. (www.randolphstreetmarket.com; 1350 W Randolph St; admission $10; 🕐 10am-5pm Sat, to 4pm Sun, last weekend of the month; M Green, Pink Line to Ashland)

Explore

South Loop & Near South Side

In the South Loop, the world-renowned Field Museum and other top institutions huddle at the Museum Campus. Tranquil 12th St Beach and Northerly Island, a prairie-grassed nature park, offer escapes if the crowds get to be too much. Historic buildings dot the area, including Chess Records, the seminal blues label. Chicago's small but busy Chinatown is also here.

SHEDD AQUARIUM
THERESA / CARBBONOAM /GETTY IMAGES ©

The Sights in a Day

Spend the morning at the Museum Campus, and take your pick of the big-ticket sights. The **Field Museum of Natural History** (p112) offers dinosaurs, mummies and gemstones; the **Adler Planetarium** (p116) has telescopes and starry films.

Stay on at the Museum Campus and explore nearby **Northerly Island** (p116) and **12th Street Beach** (p117). **Lou Malnati's** (p118) makes a fine refueling stop. Blues diehards should make the pilgrimage to **Willie Dixon's Blues Heaven** (p117). The beer garden at **Spoke & Bird** (p119) is a splendid way to blow the rest of the afternoon.

If it's Friday, Saturday or Sunday, put on your dancing shoes and groove to world beats at **SummerDance** (p120). Share tapas for dinner at convivial **Mercat a la Planxa** (p118). See who's bending frets at **Buddy Guy's Legends** (p120), the iconic bluesman's club and the city's best for the genre. If jazz is your sound, head to **Jazz Showcase** (p120) for a top-tier show.

 Top Sights

Field Museum of Natural History (p112)

 Best of Chicago

Museums & Galleries
Adler Planetarium (p116)

Museum of Contemporary Photography (p116)

Field Museum of Natural History (p112)

Live Music
Buddy Guy's Legends (p120)

Jazz Showcase (p120)

Parks & Gardens
Northerly Island (p116)

Comedy & Performing Arts
SummerDance (p120)

Sports & Activities
Chicago Bears (p120)

Getting There

M **El** Red Line to Harrison and Red, Orange, Green Line to Roosevelt for South Loop.

Bus Numbers 130 (in summer) and 146 (year-round) go to the Museum Campus.

Top Sights
Field Museum of Natural History

The mammoth Field Museum houses everything but the kitchen sink – beetles, mummies, gemstones, Bushman the stuffed ape. The collection's rock star is Sue, the largest Tyrannosaurus rex yet discovered. She's 13ft tall, 41ft long, and she menaces the main floor with ferocious aplomb. The galleries beyond hold 20 million other artifacts, tended by a slew of PhD-wielding scientists, as the Field remains an active research institution.

👁 Map p114, C4

📞312-922-9410

www.fieldmuseum.org

1400 S Lake Shore Dr

adult/child $18/13

🕑9am-5pm

🚌146, 130

Dinosaur skeleton model, Field Museum of Natural History

Don't Miss

Dinosaur Stash

After communing with Sue, dino lovers should head up to the Evolving Planet exhibit on the 2nd floor, which has more of the big guys and gals. You can learn about the evolution of the species and watch staff paleontologists clean up fossils in the lab. There's even a mask that lets you see the world through a trilobite's eyes.

Mummies Galore

'Inside Ancient Egypt' is another good exhibit that re-creates an Egyptian burial chamber on three levels. The mastaba (tomb) contains 23 actual mummies and is a reconstruction of the one built for Unis-ankh, the son of the last pharaoh of the Fifth dynasty, who died at age 21 in 2407 BC. The bottom level, with its twisting caverns, is especially worthwhile.

Gems & Stuffed Animals

Other displays that merit your time include the Hall of Gems and its glittering garnets, opals, pearls and deep-blue tanzanite stones (1000 times rarer than diamonds, which you'll also see plenty of). The Northwest Coast and Arctic Peoples totem pole collection got its start with artifacts shipped to Chicago for the 1893 World's Expo. And the largest man-eating lion ever caught is stuffed and standing sentry on the basement floor. Preserved insects, birds and Bushman, the cantankerous ape who drew crowds at Lincoln Park Zoo for decades, are also on display in all their taxidermic glory.

☑ Top Tips

▶ Ask for the 'Basic' admission to see everything mentioned here.

▶ The All Access and Discovery admission tickets include extras such as the 3D movie and special exhibits, which can be too much if you're doing lots of sightseeing.

▶ The museum is vast, so get a map at the desk and make a plan of attack to see your top exhibits.

▶ The various shops inside are worth a browse for their abundant dino gear and educational toys.

✕ Take a Break

Chomp into the deep-dish pizza at Lou Malnati's (p118), an originator of the genre. The beer garden at Spoke & Bird (p119) beckons for locally sourced sandwiches and brews.

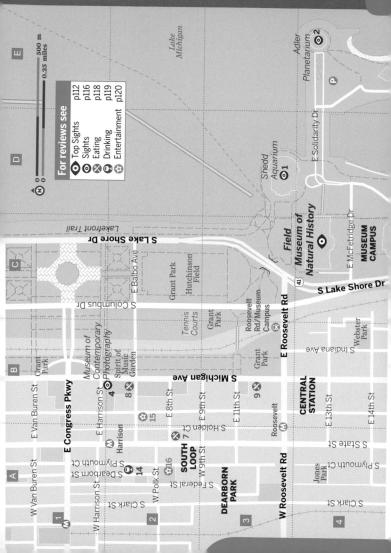

For reviews see

Lake Michigan

Adler Planetarium

Shedd Aquarium

Field Museum of Natural History

MUSEUM CAMPUS

E Solidarity Dr

E McFetridge Dr

S Lake Shore Dr

Lakefront Trail

S Lake Shore Dr

Grant Park

Hutchinson Field

Grant Park

Tennis Courts

Grant Park

Roosevelt Rd/Museum Campus

E Roosevelt Rd

Columbus Dr

E Balbo Ave

Museum of Contemporary Photography

Spirit of Music Garden

S Michigan Ave

E Van Buren St

E Congress Pkwy

E Harrison St

E 8th St

E 9th St

E 11th St

S Indiana Ave

Webster Park

CENTRAL STATION

E 13th St

E 14th St

W Van Buren St

S Clark St

W Harrison St

S Plymouth Ct

S Dearborn St

Harrison

W Polk St

W 9th St

S Holden Ct

SOUTH LOOP

S Federal St

DEARBORN PARK

W Roosevelt Rd

Roosevelt

S State St

S Plymouth Ct

Jones Park

S Clark St

500 m
0.25 miles

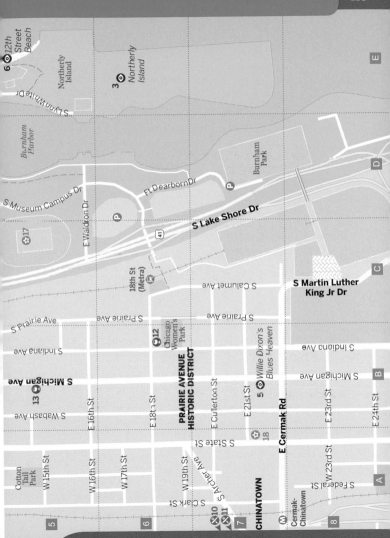

6 12th Street Beach

Northerly Island

3 Northerly Island

S Lynn White Dr

Burnham Harbor

Burnham Park

Ft Dearborn Dr

S Museum Campus Dr

E Waldron Dr

S Lake Shore Dr

17

18th St (Metra)

41

S Calumet Ave

S Prairie Ave

S Prairie Ave

S Prairie Ave

S Martin Luther King Jr Dr

S Indiana Ave

S Indiana Ave

12 Chicago Women's Park

S Michigan Ave

13 S Michigan Ave

S Michigan Ave

S Wabash Ave

E 16th St

E 18th St

PRAIRIE AVENUE HISTORIC DISTRICT

E Cullerton St

E 21st St

5 Willie Dixon's Blues Heaven

E Cermak Rd

18

S State St

E 23rd St

E 24th St

Cotton Tail Park

W 15th St

W 16th St

W 17th St

S Archer Ave

W 19th St

E Cermak Rd

W 23rd St

S Federal St

S Clark St

CHINATOWN

Cermak-Chinatown

10
11

7

8

5

6

7

8

Sights

Shedd Aquarium
AQUARIUM

1 Map p114, D3

Top draws at the kiddie-mobbed Shedd Aquarium include the Wild Reef exhibit, where there's just 5in of Plexiglas between you and two dozen fierce-looking sharks, and the Oceanarium, with its rescued sea otters. Note the Oceanarium also keeps beluga whales and Pacific white-sided dolphins, a practice that has become increasingly controversial in recent years. (☑312-939-2438; www.sheddaquarium.org; 1200 S Lake Shore Dr; adult/child $31/22; ⏱9am-5pm Mon-Fri, to 6pm Sat & Sun Sep-May, to 6pm daily Jun-Aug; 👪; ☒146, 130)

✓ Top Tip

Shedd Aquarium Savings

For the Shedd Aquarium, there is a little-advertised option to buy a 'general admission' ticket for $8 ($6 for children). This allows you to see the basic tanks of fish, turtles and eels, but no sharks, sea otters or other more exotic creatures. Alas, you cannot buy general admission tickets in advance, which can be a problem in summer when Shedd queues are long (as pre-bought tickets provide faster, priority entry).

Adler Planetarium
MUSEUM

2 Map p114, E4

Space enthusiasts will get a big bang (pun!) out of the Adler. There are public telescopes to view the stars, 3D lectures to learn about supernovas and the Planet Explorers exhibit where kids can 'launch' a rocket. The immersive digital films cost $13 extra. The Adler's front steps offer Chicago's best skyline view. (☑312-922-7827; www.adlerplanetarium.org; 1300 S Lake Shore Dr; adult/child $12/8; ⏱9:30am-4pm Mon-Fri, to 4:30 Sat & Sun; 👪; ☒146, 130)

Northerly Island
PARK

3 Map p114, E6

The prairie-grassed park has walking trails, fishing, bird-watching and an outdoor venue for big-name concerts (which you can hear from 12th St Beach). (1400 S Lynn White Dr; ☒146 or 130)

Museum of Contemporary Photography
MUSEUM

4 Map p114, B2

This museum focuses on American photography since 1937, and is the only institution of its kind between the coasts. The permanent collection includes the works of Debbie Fleming Caffery, Mark Klett, Catherine Wagner, Patrick Nagatani and 500 more of the best photographers working today. Special exhibitions (also free) augment the rotating permanent collection. (☑312-663-5554; www.mocp.org; 600

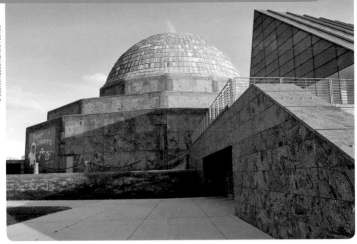

BRUCE LEIGHTY/GETTY IMAGES ©

Adler Planetarium

S Michigan Ave, Columbia College; admission free; ⊙10am-5pm Mon-Wed, Fri & Sat, to 8pm Thu, noon-5pm Sun; Ⓜ Red Line to Harrison)

Willie Dixon's Blues Heaven
HISTORIC BUILDING

5 ⊙ Map p114, B7

From 1957 to 1967, this humble building was Chess Records, the seminal electric blues label. It's now named for the bassist who wrote most of Chess's hits. Staff give hour-long tours of the premises. It's pretty ramshackle, with few original artifacts on display. Still, when Willie's grandson hauls out the bluesman's well-worn standup bass and lets you take a pluck, it's pretty cool. (🕿312-808-1286; www.bluesheaven.

com; 2120 S Michigan Ave; tours $10; ⊙noon-4pm Mon-Fri, to 3pm Sat; Ⓜ Green Line to Cermak-McCormick Pl)

12th Street Beach
BEACH

6 ⊙ Map p114, E5

A path runs south from the Adler Planetarium to this secluded crescent of sand. Despite its proximity to the visitor-mobbed Museum Campus, the beach remains bizarrely (but happily) secluded. Bonus: if you can't get tickets to see your favorite band at the Pavilion at Northerly Island, you can sit here and still hear the tunes. (www.cpdbeaches.com; 1200 S Linn White Dr; 🚍146, 130)

Eating

Lou Malnati's

PIZZA $

 7 Map p114, A2

Lou Malnati's is one of the city's premier deep-dish pizza makers. In fact, it claims to having invented the gooey behemoth (though that's a matter of never-ending dispute). Not in dispute: the deliciousness of Malnati's famed butter crust. Gluten-free diners can opt for the sausage crust (it's literally just meat, no dough). The restaurant has outlets citywide. (312-786-1000; www.loumalnatis.com; 805 S State St; small pizzas from $12; 11am-11pm Sun-Thu, to midnight Fri & Sat; M Red Line to Harrison)

Mercat a la Planxa

SPANISH $$$

 8 Map p114, B2

This Barcelona-style tapas and seafood restaurant buzzes in an enormous, convivial room where light streams in the floor-to-ceiling windows. *Iron Chef* winner Jose Garces cooks all the specialties of Catalan and stokes a festive atmosphere, enhanced by copious quantities of cava (sparkling wine) and sangria. It's located in the beaux arts Blackstone Hotel. (312-765-0524; www.mercatchicago.com; 638 S Michigan Ave; tapas $10-17, tasting menus from $65; 6:30am-10pm Mon-Thu, to 11pm Fri, 7am-11pm Sat, to 10pm Sun; M Red Line to Harrison)

Yolk

BREAKFAST $

 9 Map p114, B3

This cheerful diner is worth the long wait – you'll dig into the best traditional breakfast in the South Loop. The omelets include lots of healthy options (the Iron Man is made from egg whites and comes loaded with veggies and avocado), and sweets lovers have stacks of cinnamon-roll French toast and peach-cobbler crepes to drench in syrup. (312-789-9655; www.eatyolk.com; 1120 S Michigan Ave; mains $10-14; 6am-3pm Mon-Fri, from 7am Sat & Sun; M Red, Orange, Green Line to Roosevelt)

Sweet Station

CHINESE $

 10 Map p114, A7

Join the young, hip Asian crowd chowing at Sweet Station in Chinatown Sq. Slide into a booth, flip on the table's flat-screen TV, then settle in to examine the massive menu. It sprawls through a global medley including Portuguese pork chop sandwiches, Hong Kong–style baked spaghetti, Szechuan hot pots, curried tofu and good ol' French toast. Open late. (312-842-2228; www.mysweetstation.com; 2101 S China Pl; mains $5-10; 8am-4am Mon-Thu, 24hr Fri & Sat, to 2am Sun; M Red Line to Cermak-Chinatown)

Joy Yee's Noodle Shop ASIAN $

11 Map p114, A7

Folks line up for bubble teas packed with fresh fruit at this brightly colored, hip cafe in Chinatown Sq. Do yourself a favor, though, and save one of the deliciously sweet drinks for dessert after a bowl of udon, *chow fun* (rice noodles) or chow mein. (312-328-0001; www.joyyeechicago.com; 2139 S China Pl; mains $9-15; ⊙11am-10:30pm; Red Line to Cermak-Chinatown)

Drinking

Spoke & Bird CAFE

12 Map p114, B6

The South Loop has been begging for a leafy patio like the one at Spoke & Bird. Bonus: it's surrounded by several stately old manors in the Prairie Avenue Historic District. Relax with a locally made brew (as in made down the street) and nifty cafe fare like the sweet parsnip muffin or lamb barbecue sandwich. (www.spokeandbird.com; 205 E 18th St; ⊙7am-6pm; 📶1)

Vice District Brewing MICROBREWERY

13 Map p114, B5

Vice opened in 2014 and has quickly become a South Loop favorite. The large, mod-industrial taproom is just right for a pint of black IPA or

Top Tip

Free Blues Concerts

Buddy Guy's Legends (p120) hosts free, all-ages acoustic performances from noon to 2pm Wednesday through Sunday. Listen in while having lunch (the club doubles as a Cajun restaurant) or a drink at the bar. Free blues concerts also rock the side garden at **Willie Dixon's Blues Heaven** (p117) on Thursdays at 6pm in summer.

English-style bitter ale. Many drinkers stop in for pre–Bears game drinks. It's not far from Soldier Field, and it opens early – at 11am – on Sunday game days. (www.vicedistrictbrewing.com; 1454 S Michigan Ave; ⊙4-11pm Tue-Thu, to 1am Fri, noon-1am Sat, 2-9pm Sun; Green, Orange, Red Line to Roosevelt)

Kasey's Tavern PUB

14 Map p114, A2

Kasey's is a friendly neighborhood pub that draws a mix of artsy students from the nearby universities, local condo dwellers and sports fans, all of whom belly up at the long wooden bar. There's something for everyone on the enormous beer list. Scads of flat-screen TVs show Chicago's sports teams in action. (www.kaseystavern.com; 701 S Dearborn St; ⊙11am-2am; Red Line to Harrison)

Local Life
SummerDance

To boogie with a multiethnic mash-up of locals, head to the Spirit of Music Garden in Grant Park for **SummerDance** (Map p114, B2; www.chicagosummerdance.org; 601 S Michigan Ave; admission free; ⏰6-9:30pm Fri & Sat, 4-7pm Sun late Jun–mid-Sep; Ⓜ Red Line to Harrison). Bands play rumba, samba and other world beats preceded by fun dance lessons – all free. Ballroom-quality moves are absolutely not required.

Entertainment

Buddy Guy's Legends   BLUES
15 ⭐ Map p114, B2

Top local and national acts wail on the stage of local icon Buddy Guy. Tickets cost $20 Friday and Saturday, $10 on other evenings. The man himself usually plugs in his axe for a series of shows in January (tickets go on sale in November). The location is a bit rough around the edges, but the acts are consistently excellent. (www.buddyguy.com; 700 S Wabash Ave; ⏰5pm-2am Mon & Tue, 11am-2am Wed-Fri, noon-3am Sat, noon-2am Sun; Ⓜ Red Line to Harrison)

Jazz Showcase   JAZZ
16 ⭐ Map p114, A2

The Jazz Showcase, set in a gorgeous room in historic Dearborn Station, is Chicago's top club for national names. In general, local musicians take the stage Monday through Wednesday, with visiting jazz cats blowing their horns Thursday through Sunday. (www.jazzshowcase.com; 806 S Plymouth Ct; ⏰from 8pm Mon-Sat, from 4pm Sun; Ⓜ Red Line to Harrison)

Chicago Bears   FOOTBALL
17 ⭐ Map p114, C5

Da Bears, Chicago's NFL team, tackle at Soldier Field, recognizable by its classical-meets-flying-saucer architecture. Expect beery tailgate parties, sleet and snow. The season runs September through January. If you can't score a ticket, hit one of the South Loop bars to watch the game. (www.chicagobears.com; 1410 S Museum Campus Dr; 🚌146, 128)

Reggies Rock Club   LIVE MUSIC
18 ⭐ Map p114, A7

Bring on the punk and the all-ages shows. Graffitied Reggies books mostly touring hardcore bands at the Rock Club. Next door, Reggies Music Joint is for folks 21 and older, and hosts more mainstream (we use that term loosely) live music nightly, as well as bus trips to see the White Sox, the Bears and other sports teams. (📞312-949-0121; www.reggieslive.com; 2109 S State St; ⏰11am-2am; Ⓜ Green Line to Cermak-McCormick Pl)

Understand

Sounds of Chicago

– –

Blues

Chicago's most famous musical style comes in one color: blue. After the Great Migration of African Americans out of the rural South, Delta bluesmen set up on Chicago's street corners and in the open-air markets of Maxwell St during the 1930s. That's when Robert Johnson first recorded 'Sweet Home Chicago.' What distinguishes Chicago's regional blues style from Johnson's original ode is simple: volume. Chicago blues is defined by electric guitars plugged in to amplifiers. Muddy Waters and Howlin' Wolf were the first to create the new sound. Bluesmen from the 1950s and '60s such as Willie Dixon, Junior Wells and Elmore James, and later champions like Buddy Guy, Koko Taylor and Otis Rush, became national stars of the genre.

House

Chicago's other big taste-making musical export took root in the early '80s at a now-defunct West Loop nightclub called the Warehouse. The venue's DJ, Frankie Knuckles, got tired of spinning disco and added samples of European electronic music and beats from that new-fangled invention, the stand-alone drum machine. And so house music was born (named after Knuckles' club). Uninterested in appealing to commercial radio, the tracks used deep, pounding bass beats and instrumental samples made for dancing. House music DJs such as Derrick Carter and Larry Heard revolutionized the form and huge second-wave stars such as Felix Da Housecat, DJ Sneak and acid-house artist Armando took Chicago's thump worldwide.

Jazz & Rock

The Great Migration also helped the city become a jazz hotbed, especially in the 1920s. Louis Armstrong and Earl 'Fatha' Hines were part of the house band at the famed Sunset Cafe in Bronzeville (now Meyers Ace Hardware store, but with many of the club's original elements intact). Chicago still fosters an active, avant-garde scene. In recent decades the underground rock community has filled an important niche. Local record labels such as Touch and Go, Bloodshot and Thrill Jockey popped up in the 1980s and '90s, and the city became a hub for post-rock, alt country and noise rock bands. The reigning kings of Chicago rock are (arguably) still Wilco.

Local Life
A Bookish Day in Hyde Park

Getting There

🚌 Number 10 from Michigan Ave to MSI during museum hours; otherwise bus 6 from State St.

Ⓜ Electric Line from Loop's Millennium Station to 51st-53rd or 55th-56th-57th stops.

The University of Chicago and its grand Gothic buildings dominate Hyde Park. Faculty and students have racked up more than 80 Nobel Prizes within those hallowed halls. So it's no surprise a ramble here involves brainy bookstores and make-you-think museums, with the neighborhood's favorite dive bar and soul-food cafe thrown in for good measure.

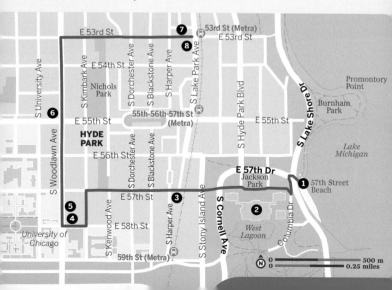

❶ 57th Street Beach

Just across Lake Shore Dr from the Museum of Science and Industry, **57th Street Beach** (www.cpdbeaches.com; 5700 S Lake Shore Dr) is a mellow stretch of sand where neighborhood families and college kids come to hit the waves. Surfers say it's the best beach to hang ten.

❷ Museum of Science & Industry

Geek out at the **Museum of Science & Industry** (www.msichicago.org; 5700 S Lake Shore Dr; adult/child $18/11; ⏰9:30am-5:30pm Jun-Aug, reduced hours Sep-May), the western hemisphere's largest science collection. Highlights include a WWII German U-boat ($9 extra to tour) and the 'Science Storms' mock tornado.

❸ Powell's

Used bookstore **Powell's** (www.powells-chicago.com; 1501 E 57th St; ⏰9am-11pm) can get you just about any title ever published. Shelf after heaving shelf prop up the well-arranged stock. Staff often put a box of tattered free books outside by the entrance.

❹ Robie House

Of the numerous buildings that Frank Lloyd Wright designed around Chicago, none is more famous or influential than **Robie House** (www.flwright.org; 5757 S Woodlawn Ave; adult/child $17/14; ⏰10:30am-3pm Thu-Mon), his horizontal-lined, Prairie-style masterwork. Inside are 174 stained-glass windows and doors, which you'll see on the hour-long tours (frequency varies by season).

❺ Seminary Co-op Bookstore

At awesomely academic **Seminary Co-op Bookstore** (www.semcoop.com; 5751 S Woodlawn Ave; ⏰8:30am-8pm Mon-Fri, 10am-6pm Sat, noon-6pm Sun), you might run into a Nobel laureate or three. Local scholars adore this place, where you'll find no less than eight versions of *War and Peace* on the shelves.

❻ Jimmy's Woodlawn Tap

Jimmy's Woodlawn Tap (1172 E 55th St; ⏰10:30am-2am Mon-Fri, from 11am Sat & Sun) is dark and beery, and a little seedy. But for thousands of University of Chicago students deprived of a thriving bar scene, it's home. Hungry? The Swissburgers are legendary.

❼ Valois Cafeteria

The neighborhood clientele at **Valois** (1518 E 53rd St; mains $5-11; ⏰5:30am-10pm) is so socioeconomically diverse that a U of C sociology professor wrote a book about it, titled *Slim's Table*. It seems Southern-style catfish, biscuits and pot pies attract all kinds – even Barack Obama, who chowed here regularly when he lived nearby.

❽ Promontory

The **Promontory** (www.promontorychicago.com; 5311 S Lake Park Ave) is Hyde Park's first hipster music hall. The rustic, huge-window room hosts jazz, soul and funk musicians, as well as DJs several nights a week. Even if there's no show, you can have a glass of wine at the bar and munch a wood-oven-roasted veggie sandwich.

The Best of
Chicago

Chicago's Best Walks

Chicago's Best...

Anish Kapoor, *Cloud Gate*, 2004 (p25)
GEOFF LIVINGSTON/GETTY IMAGES ©; ANISH KAPOOR © DACS/LICENSED BY VISCOPY, 2015

Best Walks
Skyscrapers & Street Art

🏃 The Walk

It's hard to know what to gawk at first. High-flying architecture is everywhere, thanks to Mrs O'Leary's cow (who kicked over the lantern that burned down the city in 1871, and created the blank canvas for lofty new designs). Whimsical public art adds to the eye-candy. This tour swoops through the Loop, taking in the best of it all, from sky-high record breakers to art-deco landmarks, a pink flamingo and shiny Bean, plus a visit to Al Capone's dentist thrown in for good measure.

Start Daley Plaza; Blue Line to Washington

Finish Willis Tower; Brown, Orange, Purple, Pink Line to Quincy

Length 1.25 miles; one hour

🍴 Take a Break

Fortify with a glass of wine and uber-rich dessert in the cool, clubhouse-like space of Seven Lions (p36).

Willis Tower (p30), from Lake Shore Drive

GHORNEPHOTO/GETTY IMAGES ©

❶ Picasso's Untitled

Picasso's abstract **Untitled** sculpture is ensconced in Daley Plaza. The artist never would say what the 1967 iron work represents. Most people believe it's the head of a woman. But Picasso also drew pictures of his dog that look similar. Go ahead and climb on it.

❷ Reliance Building

Head to the corner of Washington and State Sts and check out the shimmering 1890s **Reliance Building**. Its lightweight frame made it the precedent for the modern skyscraper. Today it houses the chic Hotel Burnham. Added historical bonus: Al Capone's dentist drilled teeth in what's now room 809.

❸ Chicago Cultural Center

The 1897 **Chicago Cultural Center** (p34) is a beaux arts beauty in its own right, but you're here to get inspiration from the architectural photos in the 1st-floor Landmark Gallery. The exhibit shows 72 black-and-white images of prominent structures, including several that have since been demolished.

❹ The Bean

Make your way into Millennium Park and view the silvery sculpture everyone calls 'the Bean'. Artist Anish Kapoor officially titled it **Cloud Gate**, but no matter. Join the masses swarming it to see the skyline reflect.

❺ Art Institute of Chicago

The **Art Institute** (p28) is one of Chicago's most-visited attractions,

and the 1894 bronze lions out front are city mascots of sorts. They remain regal and dignified even when the museum plops fiberglass Blackhawks helmets on their heads during Stanley Cup wins.

❻ Flamingo

Alexander Calder's **Flamingo** gives a bit of color and contrast to famed architect Ludwig Mies van der Rohe's blocky, black Kluczynski Building behind it. The 'bird' is comprised of 50 tons of bright red steel.

❼ Chicago Board of Trade

The **Board of Trade** is a 1930 art-deco gem. Inside, traders swap futures and options (something to do with corn and pork). Outside, a giant statue of Ceres, the goddess of agriculture, tops the 45-story edifice.

❽ Willis Tower

The **Willis Tower** (p30) is Chicago's tallest skyscraper, reaching 1450 ft into the heavens. Ascend to the 103rd-floor Skydeck to look over the high-rises and artworks you've just traversed.

Best Walks
Mansions, Beaches & Greenery

The Walk

The Gold Coast and Lincoln Park are among Chicago's most prized bits of real estate, but they didn't start that way. The former was a swamp, the latter a cemetery circa 1865. That changed when Lake Shore Dr opened, and Bertha and Potter Palmer built a manor at its edge. So began a rush of Chicago's wealthy to the neighborhood. The park became their fashionable playground (the cemetery was moved). This walk explores the area's past and present.

Start Original Playboy Mansion; Red Line to Clark/Division

Finish Caldwell Lily Pool; bus 151

Length 3 miles; 2½ hours

Take a Break

The **Patio at Cafe Brauer** (☏312-507-9053; 2021 N Stockton Dr; mains $8-12; ⏰11am-9pm Mon-Thu, from 8:30am Fri-Sun) is perfect for a glass of wine while sitting by the zoo's South Pond.

ED RICE/GETTY IMAGES ©

Lincoln Park Zoo (p72)

❶ Original Playboy Mansion

Hugh Hefner began wearing his all-day jammies at this 1927 **mansion** (p63), when the rigors of magazine production and partying prevented him from getting dressed. The building contains condos now, so you can't go inside. But you can let your imagination run wild about the parties that used to take place here.

❷ Astor Street

Head east a block to **Astor Street**. It was named for John Jacob Astor, one of the USA's richest citizens when he died in 1848. Astor never lived here, but the area's builders thought his name added dazzle. Several turn-of-the-century mansions rise up between the 1300 and 1500 blocks.

❸ Charnley-Persky House

While he was still working for famed architect Louis Sullivan, Frank Lloyd Wright (who was 19 at the time) designed the **Charnley-Persky House**. It was completed in 1892 and now houses the Society of Architectural Historians.

④ North Avenue Beach

Head northeast through the park (past the bikeshare, then toward the underpass) to **North Avenue Beach** (p72). It's Chicago's most popular sand lot. A short walk on the breakwater yields postcard skyline views.

⑤ Nature Boardwalk

From the beach, walk over the pedestrian bridge back into Lincoln Park. Amble around the **Nature Boardwalk**, a half-mile path around the South Pond's wetlands ecosystem.

⑥ Lincoln Park Zoo

Mosey northward through the free **zoo** (p72), which has been entertaining locals for around 150 years Zebras, snow monkeys and rhinos are among the critters that flash by.

⑦ Lincoln Park Conservatory

Continue north to the **conservatory** (p72). The fine 1891 hothouse coaxes ferns, orchids and palms to flourish.

In winter, it becomes an escape from the icy winds raging outside.

⑧ Caldwell Lily Pool

The enchanting **Caldwell Lily Pool** hides in a plot northeast of

the conservatory. It's a lovely escape from the crowd, with Prairie-style stonework, lazing turtles and dragonflies fluttering around.

Best
Architecture

The Great Fire of 1871 sparked an architectural revolution in Chicago. Daniel Burnham, one of the prime designers during the era, summed up the city's credo that lingers to this day: 'Make no little plans,' he counseled, 'for they have no magic to stir men's blood... Make big plans.' Chicago has been a hotbed for skyscrapers ever since.

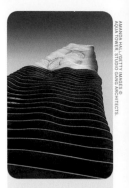

AMANDA HALL /GETTY IMAGES ©
AQUA TOWER, STUDIO GANG ARCHITECTS.

Architects to Know

You'll hear these names often as you explore the city. Louis Sullivan was Chicago's architectural founding father, a revolutionary of steel-frame high-rises. Frank Lloyd Wright was Sullivan's student, who took the Prairie style to global renown. Daniel Burnham was the man with the plan that preserved Chicago's lakefront. Ludwig Mies van der Rohe was known for his 'less is more' motto and simple, boxy designs for modern skyscrapers. Jeanne Gang is the city's current starchitect. Her mod, organic structures are popping up all over the city.

Preservation

The Chicago Architecture Foundation – known today for its great tours and gift shop – grew out of a 1960s preservation effort to save a South Loop home. The group was successful with that building, but many others met the wrecking ball. The most famous was the Stock Exchange Building, designed by Louis Sullivan and Dankmar Adler. You can still see a bit of it, as the Stock Exchange Arch was salvaged and now stands outside the Art Institute (on the northeast side). Several groups have since sprung up to ensure Chicago's worthy buildings live on.

☑ Top Tips

► For DIY explorations of Chicago's steely structures, staff at the Chicago Architecture Foundation recommend using the *Pocket Guide to Chicago Architecture* by Judith Paine McBrien, or *A View from the River*, the foundation's book that highlights buildings along its popular tour boat routes.

► The local public TV station offers a great, free mobile guide and audio tour of Loop architecture. It's available at http:/ interactive.wttw. com/loop.

Best Skyscrapers

Willis Tower Ascend 103 floors in Chicago's tallest building, then peer down from a glass-floored ledge. (p30)

360° Chicago Get high in Chicago's fourth-tallest tower at the 94th-floor observatory or 96th-floor lounge. (p56)

Tribune Tower The neo-Gothic cloud-poker is inlaid with stones from the Taj Mahal, Parthenon and more. (p48)

Marina City Groovy corn-cob towers look like something from a *Jetsons* cartoon. (p48)

Water Tower The only downtown survivor of the 1871 Great Fire was a skyscraper in its day. (p62)

Best Prairie Style

Robie House The low eves and graceful lines of Frank Lloyd Wright's masterpiece were emulated worldwide. (p123)

Rookery Wright gave the atrium a light-filled renovation that features 'floating' staircases. (p34)

Best Beaux Arts

Chicago Cultural Center Gilded ceilings, rich marble walls and mother-of-pearl mosaics bejewel the halls. (p34)

Museum of Science & Industry It was the classical Palace of Fine Arts at the landmark 1893 World's Expo. (p123)

Best Mansions

Driehaus Museum A Gilded Age manor with three floors of gorgeous decorative arts and stained glass. (p48)

Original Playboy Mansion Hugh Hefner and the Playboy bunnies used to swing in this Gold Coast beauty. (p63)

Cyrus McCormick Mansion Turn-of-the-century neoclassical home that's a relic from when Astor St was millionaires' row. (p62)

Worth a Trip

Frank Lloyd Wright Home & Studio (☏312-994-4000; www.flwright.org; 951 Chicago Ave; adult/child/camera $17/14/5; ☺10am-4pm), in suburban Oak Park, offers a fascinating, hour-long walk-through of the famed architect's abode from 1889 to 1909. It's easy to reach via the Green Line train from downtown Chicago.

Best
Eating

Chicago has become a chowhound's hot spot. The beauty here is that even the buzziest restaurants are accessible: they're visionary yet traditional, pubby at the core and decently priced. Inventive chefs have flocked in, thanks to lower costs than other big cities. So get ready: from 20-course meals of 'molecular gastronomy' to deep-dish pizza slices, this town serves up a plateful.

Local Specialties

Foremost is deep-dish pizza, with crust that rises two or three inches above the plate and cradles a molten pile of toppings. One gooey piece is practically a meal. No less iconic is the Chicago hot dog – a wiener that's been 'dragged through the garden' (ie topped with onions, tomatoes, shredded lettuce, bell peppers, pepperoncini and sweet relish, but never ketchup). The city is also revered for its spicy, drippy, only-in-Chicago Italian beef sandwiches

Eat Streets

Chicago's best and brightest chefs do their thing on Randolph St in the West Loop. Sidewalk tables spill out of bistros and cafes on Division St in Wicker Park. Mexican taquerias meet hipster hangouts along 18th St in Pilsen.

Chefs to Know

Celeb chef Rick Bayless is everywhere: on TV, cooking at the White House and tending Xoco (p49) among his various restaurants. Grant Achatz made 'molecular gastronomy' a catchphrase at Alinea (p73). Stephanie Izard gained fame as the first woman to win *Top Chef*. She now runs Girl and the Goat (p106), Little Goat (p106) and more. Native son Paul Kahan makes waves at Avec (p106) and Dove's Luncheonette (p92).

GEORGE WILHELM/GETTY IMAGES ©

☑ **Top Tips**

▶ Make dinner reservations for eateries in the midrange and upper price bracket, especially on weekends.

▶ Many restaurants let you book online through OpenTable (www.opentable.com).

▶ Need help deciding where to eat? LTH Forum (www.lthforum.com) is a great local resource.

Best for Chowhounds

Longman & Eagle Michelin-starred, shabby-chic tavern for breakfast, lunch or dinner. (p99)

Girl & the Goat Rockin' ambience and dishes starring the titular animal. (p106)

Alinea Molecular gastronomy from one of the world's best restaurants. (p73)

Publican Quality Meats Beefy sandwiches straight from the butcher's block. (p103)

Best Budget

Dove's Luncheonette Sit at the retro counter for Tex-Mex dishes, pie and whiskey. (p92)

Xoco Celeb chef Rick Bayless' Mexican street-food hut. (p49)

Irazu Chicago's lone Costa Rican eatery whips up distinctive, peppery fare. (p93)

Best Pizza

Giordano's It's like deep-dish on steroids, with awesomely bulked-up crust. (p50)

Pequod's Pizza Sweet sauce and caramelized cheese. (p74)

Pizano's Makes a great thin crust to supplement the deep dish. (p36)

Best Hot Dogs

Hot G Dog Goes beyond gourmet weenies with a killer Chicago-style dog too. (p87)

Wiener's Circle Char-dogs, cheddar fries and lots of unruly swearing. (p74)

Best Brunch

Sweet Maple Cafe Fresh-baked biscuits and banana pancakes. (p108)

Big Jones Dishes from New Orleans and the Carolina Lowcountry. (p87)

Meli Cafe Goat's cheese and fig omelets in Greektown. (p107)

Flo Hungover hipsters crave the breakfast burritos. (p94)

Best Neighborhood Gems

Hopleaf Locals pile in for the mussels, frites and 200-strong beer list. (p87)

Ruxbin Teeny spot where passionate chefs cook artful dinners. (p92)

Best Vegetarian

Mana Food Bar Swanky all-veg eatery that makes dishes from around the globe. (p93)

Handlebar Bike-messenger hangout with many meat-free dishes on the menu. (p94)

Native Foods Cafe Loop outpost of the national chain of vegan fast-casual restaurants. (p38)

Best Sweets

Hendrickx Belgian Bread Crafter Buttery waffles and dark-chocolate croissants. (p64)

La Fournette A rainbow of colorful macarons and crust-crackling baguettes. (p74)

Best
Museums &
Galleries

The world's largest Tyrannosaurus rex? The most impressionist paintings outside of France? The western hemisphere's hugest science museum? All superlatives that belong to Chicago's institutions, which draw millions of visitors each year. If big museums aren't your thing, the city has a fine assortment of smaller venues covering everything from Mexican beadwork to antique amputation saws, as well as galleries galore.

CHARLES COOK/GETTY IMAGES ©

Online Tickets

Most major museums allow you to buy tickets online. The advantage is that you're assured entry and you get to skip the regular ticket lines. The disadvantage is that you have to pay a service fee of $1.50 to $4 per ticket (sometimes it's just per order), and at times the prepay line is almost as long as the regular one. Our suggestion: consider buying online in summer and for big exhibits. Otherwise, there's no need.

Gallery Districts

Chicago has five gallery-rich zones. River North is grandfather of the scene. Top international names show off their works here; it's also the most jam-packed with galleries. The West Loop is a hotbed of edgy, avant-garde art that garners international praise. Bucktown and Wicker Park are rife with alternative spaces and emerging talent. Pilsen hosts several small, artist-run spaces that have erratic hours. And the south side neighborhood of Bridgeport has become a big player with cool-cat galleries in a warren of old warehouses on W 35th St.

☑ Top Tips

▶ The **Go Chicago Card** (www.smartdestinations.com/chicago) allows you to visit an unlimited number of attractions for a flat fee. It's good for one, two, three or five consecutive days.

▶ The company also offers a three-choice or five-choice 'Explorer Pass' where you pick among 26 options. It's valid for 30 days.

Best Art Museums

Art Institute of Chicago Gawk at Monets, modern works, miniatures and more at the nation's second-largest art museum. (p28)

Museum of Contemporary Art Consider it the Art Institute's unruly sibling: a collection that always pushes boundaries. (p58)

National Museum of Mexican Art It holds a terrific collection of classical paintings, altars, folk art and politically charged pieces. (p106)

Best Science Museums

Field Museum of Natural History Explore collections of dinosaurs, gems, mummies and enormous taxidermied lions. (p112)

Museum of Science & Industry You could spend an entire day in the western hemisphere's largest science museum. (p123)

Adler Planetarium Journey to the nether regions of outer space at this lakeside gem. (pictured left; p116)

Best Galleries

Mars Gallery It's pop art presided over by a kitty cat (he's the assistant manager). (p102)

Galerie F One-of-a-kind, rock-and-roll gallery for gig posters and street art. (p99)

Intuit: the Center for Intuitive and Outsider Art Holds a museum-quality display of folk art. (p92)

Best Offbeat Museums

International Museum of Surgical Science Amputation saws, iron lungs and a roomful of cadaver murals cram a creepy old mansion. (p62)

Money Museum You'll emerge richer than when you entered, thanks to a take-home bag of shredded currency. (p35)

Best Underappreciated Museums

Peggy Notebaert Nature Museum Hands-on, family-oriented spot with a turtle-filled marsh and butterfly garden. (p72)

Chicago History Museum Tells the city's story with artifacts such as Prohibition-era booze stills. (p72)

Museum of Contemporary Photography Tidy and engaging (and free), it's a great stop in the South Loop. (p116)

DePaul Art Museum The university's free venue hosts engaging exhibits of 20th-century works. (p73)

Worth a Trip
Bridgeport has become a pocket of artsy cool. Side-by-side **Zhou B Art Center** (www.zhoubartcenter.com; 1029 W 35th St; 8) and **Bridgeport Art Center** (www.bridgeportart.com; 1200 W 35th St; 8) revamped warehouses – hold the mother lode of galleries and workshops. The best time to visit is during the Third Friday open studios event (from 6pm to 10pm), though many galleries are open throughout the week. They're easiest to reach by car, though bus 8 along Halsted St also gets you close.

Best
Parks & Gardens

Chicago takes green space seriously. Since the 1830s its motto has been 'Urbs in horto,' Latin for 'City in a Garden.' Almost the entire lakefront is public parkland, thanks to city planner Daniel Burnham. When he pieced the city together again after the Great Fire he made sure enormous parks were part of the package.

BRUCE LEIGHTY/GETTY IMAGES ©

Best for Strolling & Lolling

Millennium Park
Meander around interactive public artworks, then bring a picnic for the evening concert. (pictured; p24)

Northerly Island The grassy park offers a tranquil escape from the nearby Museum Campus. (p116)

Best for Active Types

The 606 Old train track turned elevated path rolls for 2.7 miles through Wicker Park, Logan Square and onward. (p92)

Maggie Daley Park Blow off steam at the rock-climbing wall, ice-skating

ribbon, mini-golf course and whimsical playgrounds. (p34)

Lincoln Park Join joggers, rowers, walkers and cyclists in Chicago's largest green space. (p68)

Best for People-Watching

Buckingham Fountain
Everyone gathers around Grant Park's centerpiece for its trippy light shows and 15-story-high spout. (p34)

Mary Bartelme Park
See how the West Loop's hipsters and families get their exercise. (p103)

 **Top Tips**

▶ The website of the Chicago Park District (www.chicagoparkdistrict.com) lists all kinds of free events – movies, live music, theater – that take place in green spaces citywide.

Best Gardens

Lincoln Park Conservatory The small but potent dose of tropical blooms is especially welcome during winter. (p72)

Lurie Garden Find Millennium Park's secret garden and you're treated to a prairie's worth of wildflowers. (p26)

Best
Live Music

The birthplace of electric blues and house music, Chicago also fosters a rip-roaring indie rock scene, boundary-leaping jazz cats and all kinds of world beats. Venues are thick on the ground, with tunes spilling out of muggy clubs, sunny outdoor amphitheaters, DIY dive bars and everyplace in between.

MIKE WINDLE/GETTY IMAGES ©

Neighborhood Hubs

Wicker Park and Logan Square hold the mother lode of cool little clubs where edgy indie bands plug in. Blues and jazz clubs are scattered around town, though a couple of big-name spots pop up in the South Loop. Lincoln Park offers convenient access to blues bars (especially on Halsted St) and intimate alternative venues.

Best Blues

Buddy Guy's Legends The iconic bluesman's club puts the best bands on stage. (p120)

BLUES Small, crackling club with seasoned local players. (p76)

Kingston Mines Hot and sweaty late-night venue with two stages jamming daily. (p77)

Best Jazz

Green Mill Big names bebop in this timeless tavern where Al Capone used to chill. (p87)

Whistler Artsy little club where indie bands and jazz trios brood. (p99)

Jazz Showcase Elegant room where national acts blow their horns. (p120)

Best Rock

Hideout Feels like your grandma's basement but with alt-country bands and literary readings. (p95)

☑ Top Tips

▶ See the alt-weekly *Chicago Reader* (www.chicagoreader.com) for comprehensive listings.

Empty Bottle The city's go-to club for edgy indie rock and cheap Pabst beer. (p96)

Double Door Cool buzz bands smash through sets in this Wicker Park landmark. (pictured; p95)

Metro Bands on the way up thrash here first. (p85)

Lincoln Hall Indie bands love to play the intimate room with pristine acoustics. (p77)

Best
Sports &
Activities

Chicago is a rabid sports town, and fans of the pro teams are famously die-hard. It's not all about passively watching sports, though. Chicago offers plenty of places to get active via its city-spanning shoreline, 26 beaches and 580 parks. After a long, cold winter, everyone goes outside to play.

MIKE MCGINNIS/GETTY IMAGES ©

Lakefront Trail & Beaches

The flat, 18-mile Lakefront Trail is a beautiful route along the water, though on nice days it's jam-packed with joggers and cyclists. It also connects the city's beaches. In summer lifeguards patrol the strands of sand. Swimming is popular, though the water is pretty freaking cold.

Best Spectator Sports

Chicago Cubs It's hard to beat a day at Wrigley Field, beer in hand in the sun-splashed bleachers. (p85)

Chicago Bears Prepare your Mike Ditka mustache and get ready for a

whopping tailgate party. (p120)

Best Beaches

North Avenue Beach Party time at the boathouse and on the volleyball courts (p72)

Oak Street Beach Sand box in the shadow of skyscrapers. (p62)

Best Guided Jaunts

Bobby's Bike Hike Groovy tours for children and pizza- and beer-lovers. (p149)

Bike Chicago More excellent tours from Lincoln Park to Obama's house. (p148)

Urban Kayaks Rentals and fireworks tours launch downtown from the Riverwalk. (p35)

 Top Tips

▶ White Sox (www.whitesox.com) baseball tickets are usually cheaper and easier to get than Cubs tickets. The Sox play at US Cellular Field, 4 miles south of downtown and accessible via the El (Red Line to Sox-35th).

▶ For all teams, buy tickets direct from their website or stadium box office.

Best
Drinking &
Nightlife

Chicagoans love to hang out in drinking establishments. Blame it on the long winter, when folks need to huddle together somewhere warm. Blame it on summer, when sunny days make beer gardens and sidewalk patios so splendid. Whatever the reason, drinking in the city is a widely cherished civic pastime.

FRANZ MARC FREI/GETTY IMAGES ©

Clubs

Clubs cluster in three main areas: River North/West Loop, where the venues tend to be huge and luxurious (with dress codes); Wicker Park/Ukie Village, where they're typically more casual; and Wrigleyville/Boystown, where they fall in between the two extremes.

How to Find a Real Chicago Bar

Look for the following: an 'Old Style' beer sign swinging out front; a well-worn dart board and/or pool table inside; patrons wearing ballcaps with the logos of the Cubs, White Sox, Bears or Blackhawks; and sports on TV.

Best Overall

Old Town Ale House Trendy tipplers and grizzled regulars sip under bawdy paintings. (p75)

Revolution Brewing Industrial-chic brewpub pouring righteous ales. (p99)

Best Beer

Delilah's Spirited punk bar with all kinds of odd ales (whiskeys too). (p75)

Map Room Globe-laden tavern with 200 worldly brews. (p95)

Best Cocktails

Violet Hour Beard-award-winning cocktails in a hidden bar. (p94)

Matchbox Teensy space with big gimlets. (p95)

☑ Top Tips

▶ The alt-weekly *Chicago Reader* (www.chicagoreader.com) has complete club listings.

Best Views

Signature Lounge Ascend to the Hancock Center's 96th floor and gawp. (p64)

J Parker The lake and skyline look sweet from this Lincoln Park rooftop. (p75)

Best Clubs

Smart Bar Intimate room that's serious about its DJs. (p84)

Berlin Welcome one, welcome all space to dance your ass off. (p84)

Best For Kids

Ferocious dinosaurs at the Field Museum, an ark's worth of beasts at Lincoln Park Zoo, lakefront boat rides and sandy beaches are among the top choices for toddlin' times. Add in magical playgrounds, family cycling tours and pizza places on practically every block, and it's clear Chicago is a kid's kind of town.

STEVE SCHNEIDER/GETTY IMAGES ©

Best Museums

Chicago Children's Museum The slew of building, climbing and inventing exhibits keep young ones busy. (p49)

Museum of Science & Industry Staff conduct 'experiments', such as dropping things off balconies and creating mini-explosions. (p123)

Field Museum of Natural History The PlayLab lets tykes excavate bones and make other discoveries. (p112)

Peggy Notebaert Nature Museum The butterfly haven and marsh full of frogs provide gentle thrills. (p72)

Best Entertainment

Navy Pier The whirling swing, sky-high Ferris wheel, musical carousel – all here, plus boats and mini-golf. (pictured; p44)

Maggie Daley Park Enchanted forests and pirate-themed playgrounds. (p34)

Lincoln Park Zoo Swinging chimps, roaring lions and a barnyard full of farm animals to feed. (p72)

North Avenue Beach Pint-sized waves are perfect for pint-sized swimmers. (p72)

Best Kids' Cuisine

Shake Shack Burgers, fries and milkshakes keep it simple and delicious. (p38)

Lou Mitchell's Free candy and doughnut holes supplement the plate-defying pancakes. (p107)

☑ Top Tips

► For kid-friendly happenings around town see **Chicago Parent** (www.chicago-parent.com).

► Bobby's Bike Hike and Bike Chicago rent children's bikes and bikes with child seats. Both also offer child-friendly tours.

Best Shops

American Girl Place Have tea and get a new hair style with your doll. (p65)

Hershey's Chocolate, chocolate and more chocolate. (p65)

Lego Store So many cool things to build at the hands-on tables. (p65)

Best
Gay & Lesbian

Chicago has a flourishing gay and lesbian scene. The biggest concentration of bars and clubs is in Wrigleyville on N Halsted St between Belmont Ave and Grace St, an area known as Boystown. Andersonville is the other main area for LGBT nightlife. It's a more relaxed, less party-oriented atmosphere.

CHARLES COOK/GETTY IMAGES ©

Festivals

The main event on the calendar is the **Pride Parade** (chicagopride. gopride.com), held the last Sunday in June. It winds through Boystown and attracts more than 800,000 risqué revelers. **Northalsted Market Days** (www.northalsted.com) is another wild time in Boystown. It's a steamy two-day street fair in mid-August. Crafty, incense-wafting vendors line Halsted St, but most folks come for the drag queens in feather boas, Twister games played in the street and disco divas (Gloria Gaynor!) on the main stage. The **International Mr Leather** (www.imrl.com) contest

brings out lots of men in, well, leather in late May. Speakers, workshops and parties take place around town, with the main event happening at a downtown hotel or theater.

Sidetrack Thumping dance music, show-tune singalongs and prime people-watching. (p84)

Hamburger Mary's Cabaret, karaoke, burgers and a booze-soaked outdoor patio for good times. (p87)

Berlin For more than three decades it's where party people dance until the sun comes up. (p84)

Closet A small, laid-back bar for ladies until the boys crash late night. (p84)

Home Bistro Bring your own wine and settle in for nouveau comfort food in Boystown's center. (p83)

Best
Comedy & Performing Arts

Improv comedy was born in Chicago, and the city still nurtures the best in the biz. Chicago's reputation for stage drama is well deserved, with Hollywood-star-laden Steppenwolf among the 200 local theaters. Many productions export to Broadway, while many play in fringy 'off-Loop' storefronts. The symphony and opera also draw worldwide accolades.

RICHARD NOWITZ/GETTY IMAGES ©

Improv

Improv started in a Hyde Park bar in 1955 with the Compass Players. Their original gag was to incorporate audience suggestions into their quick-witted routine. They went on to found Second City, and their style of unstructured, spectator-fueled skits went viral.

Theater District

Chicago's Theater District is a group of century-old, neon-lit playhouses that cluster at State and Randolph Sts. They usually host big touring productions.

Best Comedy

Second City The improv bastion that launched many a career. (p76)

iO Theater Another improv house that's sent many to stardom. (p76)

ComedySportz Two teams compete for your laughs. (p85)

Best Theater

Steppenwolf Theatre Drama club of Malkovich, Sinise and other Hollywood stars. (p76)

Goodman Theatre Excellent new and classic American plays. (p40)

Best Classical & Opera

Grant Park Orchestra Everyone's favorite group to picnic with at Pritzker Pavilion. (p40)

Chicago Symphony Orchestra World-renowned, with a smokin' brass section. (p40)

☑ **Top Tips**

▶ Hot Tix (www.hot-tix.org) sells same-week drama, comedy and performing arts tickets for half-price (plus a service charge of around $4). The selection is best early in the week.

Lyric Opera High Cs in a chandeliered venue. (p40)

Best Dance

Hubbard Street Dance Chicago Foremost modern troupe in town. (p41)

SummerDance Locals young and old come out for free world-music concerts and dance lessons. (p120)

Best
Shopping

CHARLES COOK/GETTY IMAGES ©

From the glossy stores of the Magnificent Mile to the countercultural shops of Lake View to the vintage boutiques of Wicker Park, Chicago is a shopper's destination. It has been that way from the get-go. After all, this is the city that birthed the department store and traditions such as the money-back guarantee, bridal registry and bargain basement.

Specialties

Music is big. Independent record stores flood Chicago's neighborhoods, supported by the thriving live-music scene in town. Vinyl geeks will find heaps of stacks to flip through. Vintage and thrift fashions are another claim to fame. Art- and architecture-related items are also Chicago specialties.

Best Music

Jazz Record Mart One-stop shop for Chicago jazz and blues tunes. (pictured; p52)

Dusty Groove Killer stacks of vinyl hold rare soul and funk beats. (p97)

Reckless Records Great place to get the scoop on local indie rock bands. (p97)

Best Books

Quimby's Ground zero for comics, zines and underground culture. (p96)

Seminary Co-op Bookstore Brainy shop beloved by Nobel Prize winners. (p123)

Best Souvenirs

Chicago Architecture Foundation Shop Pick up a mini Willis Tower model or skyline poster. (p41)

Strange Cargo Huge array of iconic T-shirt iron-ons, from Coach Ditka to a Chicago-style hot-dog diagram. (p85)

Garrett Popcorn The sweet and salty mix will haunt your dreams. (p52)

Best Fashion & Vintage

Una Mae's Emerge looking all Jackie O in your new old hat. (p97)

Knee Deep Vintage Groovy garb and home wares from the 1920s to the 1970s. (p109)

Wolfbait & B girls Local designers sew wares on site. (p99)

Best
Tours

Chicago Architecture Foundation
(CAF; 📞 312-922-3432; www.architecture.org; 224 S Michigan Ave; tours $15-50; M Brown, Orange, Green, Purple, Pink Line to Adams) The gold-standard boat tours ($40) sail from Michigan Ave's river dock. The popular Evolution of the Skyscraper walking tours ($20) leave from the downtown Michigan Ave address. Buy tickets online or at CAF.

Chicago by Foot
(www.freetoursbyfoot.com/chicago) Guides for this pay-what-you-want walking tour offer engaging stories and historical details on different jaunts covering the Loop, Gold Coast, Lincoln Park's gangster sites and many more. Most takers pay around $10 per person.

Chicago Detours
(📞 312-350-1131; www.chicagodetours.com; tours from $26) It offers engrossing, detail-rich tours (mostly walking, but also some by bus) that take in Chicago's architecture, history and culture. The Historic Pub Crawl Tour is a popular one.

InstaGreeter
(www.chicagogreeter.com/instagreeter; 77 E Randolph St; admission free; ⏰ 10am-3pm Fri & Sat, 11am-2pm Sun; M Brown, Orange, Green, Purple, Pink Line to Randolph) It provides one-hour Loop tours on the spot from the Chicago Cultural Center visitor center. In summer, free tours of Millennium Park also depart from here daily at 11:30am and 1pm.

Chicago History Museum
(📞 312-642-4600; www.chicagohistory.org; tours $20-55; pictured) The museum counts El (elevated/subway system) jaunts, cycling routes and cemetery walks among its excellent tour arsenal. Departure points and times vary.

STEVE GEER/GETTY IMAGES ©

☑ Top Tips

▶ Many companies offer discounts if you book online.

▶ Most outdoor-oriented tours operate from April to November only.

Chicago Food Planet Tours
(📞 312-818-2170; www.chicagofoodplanet.com; 3hr tours $45-55) Go on a guided walkabout in Wicker Park, the Gold Coast or Chinatown, where you'll graze through five or more neighborhood eateries. Departure points and times vary.

Survival Guide

Survival Guide

Before You Go

When to Go

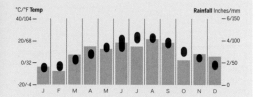

→ Winter (Dec-Feb)
December twinkles with holiday festivals. Otherwise it's gray, snowy and cold, with low-season bargains.

→ Spring (Mar-May) Still chilly, though gorgeous days sprinkle in, prime for catching a baseball game.

→ Summer (Jun-Aug)
Peak tourism season thanks to warm weather and festivals. Can be hot and humid, but usually comfy.

→ Autumn (Sep-Nov)
Shoulder season. Lodging prices decrease. Football, hockey and basketball ramp up.

Book Your Stay

☑ **Top Tip** Chicago's 16.4% hotel tax is not included in most quoted rates.

→ The Loop and Near North are the most lodging-filled neighborhoods.

→ For parking costs, figure on $55 to $65 per night downtown ($25 per night in outlying neighborhoods).

Useful Websites

→ Lonely Planet (www. lonelyplanet.com/hotels) Author-recommended reviews and online bookings.

→ Chicago Bed & Breakfast Association (www. chicago-bed-breakfast. com) Represents 15 properties.

→ Hotel Tonight (www. hoteltonight.com) National discounter with last-minute deals.

➡ **Airbnb** (www.airbnb. com) Rent a room or apartment from locals.

Best Budget

➡ **Freehand Chicago** (www.thefreehand.com/ chicago) Super-hip hostel-hotel hybrid with spiffy, high-tech dorms.

➡ **Urban Holiday Lofts** (www.urbanholidaylofts. com) It's more apartment than hostel, wafting the buzzy Bucktown vibe.

➡ **HI-Chicago** (www. hichicago.org) This hostel is reliable, immaculate and right in the Loop.

➡ **Wrigley Hostel** (www. wrigleyhostel.com) Youth-oriented hostel just spitting distance from the famed ballpark and nightlife.

Best Midrange

➡ **Acme Hotel** (www. acmehotelcompany.com) Downtown's grooviest boutique, complete with lava lights.

➡ **Wicker Park Inn** (www. wickerparkinn.com) B&B in a brick row house steps away from rockin' restaurants and nightlife.

➡ **Willows Hotel** (www. willowshotelchicago.com) Peachy rooms fill this

dapper little spot in Lake View.

➡ **Longman & Eagle** (www.longmanandeagle. com) Six wood-floored, vintage-stylish rooms that sit above a Michelin-starred gastropub.

Best Top End

➡ **Hotel Burnham** (www. burnhamhotel.com) History, architecture and yoga gear mash up in slick rooms.

➡ **Virgin Hotel** (www. virginhotels.com) The first outpost of billionaire Richard Branson's cheeky new hotel chain.

➡ **Radisson Blu Aqua Hotel** (www.radissonblu. com/aquahotel-chicago) Mod, blond-wood rooms with balconies and views.

➡ **Hotel Lincoln** (www. hotellincolnchicago.com) Fun, from 'wall of bad art' kitsch to pedicab service.

Arriving in Chicago

☑ **Top Tip** For the best way to get to your accommodations, see p17.

From O'Hare International Airport

➡ **Chicago Transit Authority** (CTA; www. transitchicago.com) The airport has its own El train station on the Blue Line. Trains run 24/7 and cost $5. They depart every 10 minutes or so and reach downtown in 40 minutes.

➡ **Airport Express** (☑888-284-3826; www.airportexpress.com) Shared van service goes downtown for $32. Vans run between 4am and 11:30pm; they leave every 15 minutes. It takes 60 minutes or more, depending on traffic and where your hotel is in the drop-off order.

➡ **Taxi** Rides to the center take 30 minutes and cost around $50. Taxi queues can be lengthy, and the ride can take longer than the train, depending on traffic.

From Chicago Midway Airport

➡ **Chicago Transit Authority** (CTA; www.transitchicago.com) The airport has its own El train station on the Orange Line. Trains operate between 4am and 1am and cost $3. They depart every 10 minutes or so and reach downtown in 30 minutes.

➡ **Airport Express** (📞888-284-3826; www.airportexpress.com) The door-to-door shuttle goes downtown for $27. Vans run between 4am and 10:30pm. It takes about 50 minutes.

➡ **Taxi** Rides to the center take 20 minutes or longer (depending on traffic) and cost $35 to $40. Taxis queue outside the main entrance.

From Union Station

➡ **Chicago Transit Authority** (CTA; www.transitchicago.com) For public transportation onward, the Blue Line Clinton stop is a few blocks south. The Brown, Orange, Purple, Pink Line station at Quincy is about a half-mile east.

➡ **Taxi** Several queue along Canal St outside the station entrance.

Getting Around

Elevated/Subway Train

☑ **Best for...** Most sights and neighborhoods.

➡ Chicago's El (it stands for 'elevated,' though many trains also run underground) is fast and frequent.

➡ Two of the eight color-coded lines – the Red Line, and the Blue Line to O'Hare airport – operate 24 hours a day. The other lines run from 4am to 1am daily.

➡ The standard fare is $3 (except from O'Hare, where it costs $5) and includes two transfers.

➡ Enter the turnstile using a Ventra Ticket, which is sold from vending machines at train stations.

➡ You can also buy a Ventra Card, aka a rechargeable fare card, at stations. It has a one-time $5 fee that gets refunded once you register the card. It knocks 50 to 75 cents off the cost of each ride.

Bus

☑ **Best for...** South Loop's Museum Campus and Lincoln Park's zoo.

➡ City buses operate from early morning until late evening.

➡ The fare is $2.25 (with a transfer).

➡ You can use a Ventra Card or pay the driver with exact change.

Bicycle

☑ **Best for...** Lincoln Park and Lakefront Trail explorations.

➡ **Divvy** (www.divvybikes.com) has 3000 sky-blue bikes at 300 stations around town.

➡ Kiosks issue 24-hour passes ($10) on the spot. Insert a credit card, get your ride code, then unlock a bike.

➡ The first 30 minutes are free; after that, rates rise fast if you don't dock the bike.

➡ Bike rentals for longer rides (with accoutrements such as helmets and locks) start at $18 per two hours. Try **Bike Chicago** (📞312-729-1000; www.bikechicago.com; 239 E Randolph St; per 1/4hr from $9/30; ⏰6:30am-10pm Mon-Fri, from 8am Sat & Sun

Jun-Aug, reduced rest of year; M Brown, Orange, Green, Purple, Pink Line to Randolph) or **Bobby's Bike Hike** (p48).

Taxi & Rideshare

☑ **Best for...** Reaching the West Loop or Pilsen from downtown, especially at night.

➜ Cabs are plentiful in the Loop, north to Andersonville and northwest to Wicker Park/Bucktown.

➜ Fares are meter-based. The meter starts at $3.25, then it's $1.80 per mile and $1 per extra passenger.

➜ Try **Yellow Cab** (☏312-829-4222; www.yellowcab-chicago.com) if you need a pick up.

➜ The rideshare company Uber is also popular in Chicago.

Car & Motorcycle

☑ **Best for...** Outlying neighborhoods.

➜ Traffic is often jammed, and street parking is scarce.

➜ Parking garages in the city cost around $38 per day.

➜ On-street, metered parking costs $2 per hour (in outlying areas)

to $6.50 per hour (in the Loop).

➜ Some meter-free streets require resident parking passes, some don't. Read the signs carefully.

Essential Information

Business Hours

Typical normal opening times are as follows:

Bars 5pm to 2am (3am on Saturday).

Nightclubs 9pm to 1am or 2am weekdays, 3am on weekends.

Saving Money on Transport

➜ If you're going to use the El more than a few times, it's worth it to buy a rechargeable Ventra Card, available at any station. You can add value as needed. Without a Ventra Card, each ride you take is subject to a surcharge for using a disposable ticket.

➜ Unlimited ride passes (one-/three-day pass $10/20) are also available; get them at railway stations.

Offices and government agencies 9am to 5pm Monday to Friday.

Restaurants Breakfast 7am or 8am to 11am, lunch 11am or 11:30am to 2:30pm, dinner 5pm or 6pm to 10pm Sunday to Thursday, to 11pm or midnight Friday and Saturday.

Shops 11am to 7pm Monday to Saturday, noon to 6pm Sunday.

Route Planner

The **Chicago Transit Authority** (www.transitchicago. com) has El and bus schedules on its website, as well as a useful trip planning feature (it basically harnesses Google).

Discount Cards

➜ The **Go Chicago Card** (www.smartdestinations.com/chicago) allows you to visit an unlimited number of attractions for a flat fee. It's good for one, two, three or five consecutive days.

➜ The company also offers a three-choice or five-choice 'Explorer Pass' where you pick among 26 options for sights. It's valid for 30 days.

➜ **CityPass** (www.citypass.com/chicago) gives access to five of the city's top draws, including the Art Institute, Shedd Aquarium and Willis Tower, over nine days. It's less flexible than Go Chicago's pass, but cheaper for those wanting a more leisurely sightseeing pace.

➜ All of these cards let you skip the regular queues at sights.

Electricity

120V/60Hz

120V/60Hz

Emergency

Police, fire and ambulance ☏911

Money

☑ **Top Tip** Tipping is not optional; only withhold tips in cases of outrageously bad service.

The US dollar ($) is the currency.

ATMs

➜ ATMs are widely available at banks, airports and convenience shops.

➜ Most ATMs link into worldwide networks (Plus, Cirrus, Exchange etc).

➜ ATMs typically charge a service fee of $3 or more per transaction.

Credit Cards

Visa, MasterCard and American Express are widely accepted at hotels, restaurants, bars and shops.

Money Exchange

Although the airports have exchange bureaus, better rates can usually be obtained at banks in the city.

Tipping

Airport & hotel porters
$2 per bag, minimum per cart $5.

Bartenders 15% per round, minimum per drink $1.

Hotel maids $2 to $5 per night.

Restaurant servers 15% to 20%, unless a gratuity is already charged on the bill.

Taxi drivers 10% to 15%, rounded up to the next dollar.

Valet parking attendants At least $2 when you're handed back the keys.

Public Holidays

Banks, schools, offices and most shops close on these days:

New Year's Day January 1

Martin Luther King Jr Day Third Monday in January

President's Day Third Monday in February

Pulaski Day First Monday in March (observed mostly by city offices)

Memorial Day Last Monday in May

Independence Day July 4

Labor Day First Monday in September

Columbus Day Second Monday in October

Veteran's Day November 11

Thanksgiving Day Fourth Thursday in November

Christmas Day December 25

Telephone

➜ **US country code** 📞1

➜ **Chicago area codes** 📞312, 773

➜ **Making international calls** Dial 📞011 + country code + area code + local number.

➜ **Calling other US area codes or Canada** Dial 📞1 + area code + seven-digit local number.

➜ **Calling within Chicago** Dial 📞1 + area code + seven-digit local number.

➜ **Cell phones** Most US cell phones – aside from iPhones – operate on CDMA, not the European standard of GSM. Be sure to double check compatibility with your phone service provider.

Tourist Information

Chicago Cultural Center Visitor Center (Map p32, E2; www.choosechicago.com; 77 E Randolph St; ⌚10am-5pm Mon-Sat, 11am-4pm Sun; 📞; Ⓜ Brown, Orange, Green, Purple, Pink Line to Randolph) It's sparse, but does offer a staffed information desk and sales of discount cards for attractions. InstaGreeter (Friday through Sunday year-round) and Millennium Park (daily in summer) tours also depart from here.

Travelers with Disabilities

➜ Most museums and major sights are wheelchair accessible, as are most large hotels and restaurants.

➜ All city buses are wheelchair accessible, but about one-third of El stations are not.

➜ **Easy Access Chicago** (www.easyaccesschicago.org) is a free resource that lists museums, tours, restaurants and lodgings, and provides mobility, vision and hearing accessibility information for each place.

Dos & Don'ts

➡ Do bring comfortable shoes, as you'll be doing a lot of walking, especially around Millennium Park and the Museum Campus.

➡ Don't smoke in restaurants or bars; Chicago is smoke-free by law in those venues.

➡ Do bring something warm to wear, as the city can get chilly even in summer.

➡ Don't worry about dressing up. It's perfectly fine to wear casual clothes to dinner or the theater.

Visas

☑ **Top Tip** Check with the US State Department (www.travel.state.gov) for updates and details on entry requirements.

➡ The Visa Waiver Program (VWP) allows nationals from 36 countries (including most EU countries, Japan, Australia and New Zealand) to enter the US without a visa for up to 90 days.

➡ VWP visitors require a machine-readable passport and approval under the Electronic System For Travel Authorization at least three days before arrival. There is a $14 fee for processing and authorization (payable online). Once approved, the registration is valid for two years.

➡ Those who need a visa – ie anyone staying longer than 90 days, or from a non-VWP country – should apply at the US consulate in their home country.

Behind the Scenes

Send Us Your Feedback

We love to hear from travelers – your comments help make our books better. We read every word, and we guarantee that your feedback goes straight to the authors. Visit **lonelyplanet.com/contact** to submit your updates and suggestions.

Note: We may edit, reproduce and incorporate your comments in Lonely Planet products such as guidebooks, websites and digital products, so let us know if you don't want your comments reproduced or your name acknowledged. For a copy of our privacy policy visit lonelyplanet.com/privacy.

Karla's Thanks

Many thanks to Alex Leviton, Kari Lydersen, Betsy Riley and Neil Anderson, Chris and Kevin Kohl, and all of my other friends who took the time to share their favorite local spots. Thanks most to Eric Markowitz, the world's best partner-for-life, who indulges all my beer- and doughnut-filled outings with an endless supply of good humor.

Acknowledgements

Cover photograph: Pritzker Pavilion, Millennium Park; Richard T. Nowitz/Corbis.

This Book

This second edition of Lonely Planet's *Pocket Chicago* guidebook was researched and written by Karla Zimmerman. The previous edition was written (as an Encounter guide) by Nate Cavalieri. This guidebook was produced by the following:

Destination Editor Dora Whitaker

Coordinating Editor Andrea Dobbin

Product Editor Joel Cotterell

Senior Cartographer David Kemp

Book Designer Katherine Marsh

Assisting Editor Justin Flynn

Cover researcher Naomi Parker

Thanks to Andi Jones, Angela Tinson, Anne Mason, Catherine Naghten, Claire Naylor, Grace Dobell, Karyn Noble, Tony Wheeler

Index

See also separate subindexes for:

⊗ **Eating p156**

⊖ **Drinking p156**

✪ **Entertainment p157**

🔒 **Shopping p157**

Sights **p000**

Map Pages **p000**

😊 Entertainment

🛍 Shopping

Our Writer

Karla Zimmerman

Karla lives in Chicago, where she has been eating deep-dish pizza (Giordano's preferred) and cheering on the hopeless Cubs for more than 25 years. Like most Chicagoans, she's more than a little keen on her home town and will talk your ear off about its sky-high architecture, global neighborhoods and character-filled dive bars. Come winter, the words she uses get a bit more colorful, especially if she's just shoveled a lot of snow. Karla writes travel content for books, magazines and websites. She has written several Lonely Planet guides covering the USA, Canada, Caribbean and Europe. Follow her on Instagram and Twitter at @karlazimmerman.

Published by Lonely Planet Publications Pty Ltd
ABN 36 005 607 983
2nd edition – Feb 2016
ISBN 9781741799026
© Lonely Planet 2016 Photographs © as indicated 2016
10 9 8 7 6 5 4 3 2 1
Printed in China